Mental Handicap

Formerly Mental Subnormality

W. Alan Heaton-Ward
MB, ChB, FRCPsych, DPM
Honorary Consultant Psychiatrist
Stoke Park Hospital Group, Bristol

Yvonne Wiley
MB, BCh, BAO, MRCPsych, DPM
Consultant Psychiatrist
Stoke Park Hospital Group, Bristol
Senior Lecturer in Mental Handicap
University of Bristol

Fifth Edition

WRIGHT
BRISTOL
1984

Published by:

John Wright & Sons Ltd, 823–825 Bath Road, Bristol BS4 5NU, England.

First edition, 1960
Reprinted, 1961
Second edition, 1963
Reprinted, 1966
Third edition, 1967
Fourth edition, 1975
Reprinted, 1976
Reprinted, 1981
Reprinted, 1983
Fifth edition, 1984

British Library Cataloguing in Publication Data
Heaton-Ward, W. Alan
    Mental Handicap.—5th ed.
    1. Mental deficiency
    I. Title   II. Wiley, Yvonne
    III. Heaton-Ward, W. Alan.   Mental
    Subnormality
    616.85′88   RC570

ISBN 0 7236 0774 5

Library of Congress Catalog Card Number: 84–50012

Printed and bound in Great Britain
by Billing & Sons Limited, Worcester.

To the memory of
my friend and teacher
Dr John Francis Lyons

W. A. H-W.

Preface to the Fifth Edition

Since the fourth edition of this book was published in 1975, the story has once again been one of steady progress rather than dramatic discoveries in our understanding of the aetiology, prevention and treatment of mental handicap. During this period, the reorientation of the general care of the mentally handicapped has continued to move outside of hospital to the community it serves. As will be described later, hospitals are developing more clearly defined roles in meeting the special needs of the mentally handicapped, which cannot be adequately met in the community. They are therefore an essential part of community services and not, as so often portrayed, a desperate last resort. Large hospitals are being reduced in size as are the individual units within them. Figures available from the Department of Health and Social Security show that, at December 1981, there were 43091 patients resident in hospitals for the mentally handicapped, compared with 58850 in 1969. Of the 1981 total, 1994 of the patients were under 16 years of age and 41097 over that age. Of the latter figure 6567 patients were aged 65 or over. By March 1982, the total number of places for the occupation and training of mentally handi-capped adults in local authority adult-training centres had increased to 45152 from the figure of 26840 quoted in *Mind Report No. 11,* published in October 1973. The Command White Paper 4683, *Better Services for the Mentally Handicapped,* published by the DHSS in June 1971, estimated a need for a further 4000 places for the residential care of children in the community and a further 31950 similar places for adults. The DHSS figure of 11077 local authority residential places for the mentally handicapped of all ages shows how far community provision still falls short of the White Paper estimate. Approximately 4800 additional residential places are provided in the community by non-statutory organizations.

While welcoming the avoidance of the unnecessary admission of any mentally handicapped person to hospital, the authors are concerned at the number of less severely handicapped who are inadequately supported in the community and who find their way to unsatisfactory accommodation, including prison, often for relatively minor offences. The authors believe that, in the enthusiasm to empty hospitals, their former 'asylum' function—in the best sense of providing a sheltered environment for such people—should not be lost. They are reinforced in this belief by the apparent support of many relatives of the mentally handicapped for the various village communities—the natural successors of the old mental deficiency colonies—which have been established by voluntary organizations around the country.

This is the first edition published under joint authorship and it gives the senior author very great pleasure to welcome Dr Yvonne Wiley in the knowledge that this well-established textbook, now in its 24th year, will enjoy a very active middle age!

Acknowledgements

The authors are grateful to the many people who have sent them reprints of their own papers, which have been invaluable in preparing this new edition, and, as always, to Dr Jozé Jancar for his constant support and helpful discussions on many of the topics in this book and to Dr Alan McDermott for advice on cytogenetics. They are grateful to Dr Pamela Mason, Dr David Primrose and Dr Brian Scally for their advice on the legal section of the book. They wish to thank, also, Mrs Joy Fearnley-Taylor for deciphering the handwriting of both authors and for typing the manuscript.

W. Alan Heaton-Ward
Yvonne Wiley

Contents

The Concept of Mental Handicap

The Mental Health Act 1959 recognized two degrees of mental subnormality: severe subnormality and subnormality. However, in all but purely legal documents these terms were replaced in daily use by 'severe mental handicap' and 'mental handicap' respectively as being more acceptable to the relatives of affected individuals. In the Mental Health Act 1983 the terms 'severe subnormality' and 'subnormality' are replaced by 'severe mental impairment' and 'mental impairment'.

Severe mental impairment is defined as 'a state of arrested or incomplete development of mind which includes *severe* impairment of intelligence and social functioning and is associated with abnormally aggressive or seriously irresponsible conduct on the part of the person concerned'.

Mental impairment is defined as 'a state of arrested or incomplete development of mind (not amounting to severe impairment) which includes *significant* impairment of intelligence and social functioning and is associated with abnormally agressive or seriously irresponsible conduct on the part of the person concerned'.

It will be seen that these definitions are much narrower than their predecessors, 'severe subnormality' and 'subnormality' and that, to be subject to the 1983 Mental Health Act, it has to be shown that the person concerned behaves in the abnormally aggressive or seriously irresponsible way which is the main requirement for the classification of mentally disordered people of normal intelligence as suffering from psychopathic disorder. As in the 1959 Mental Health Act, the definitions make no attempt to explain what is meant by 'mind'. As before, in specifying 'a state of arrested or incomplete development of mind' in each case, they make it clear that both degrees of mental impairment are to include both the cases where potentially normal mental development is arrested at some stage by environmental factors, such as injury or disease, and those cases where the potential for normal development has never been present from the time of conception owing to genetic defects. Again, the definitions make no attempt to explain what is meant by 'impairment of intelligence' nor the distinction between 'severe' and 'significant' impairment.

The authors believe that the term 'mental handicap' is a more generally acceptable and better one for describing the full range of

1

disabilities which are associated with amentia than the term 'mental impairment', as narrowly defined in the Mental Health Act, 1983. They have therefore chosen Mental Handicap as the title of this new edition and throughout the book the terms 'mental handicap' and 'severe mental handicap' are used as synonymous with 'subnormality' and 'severe subnormality' in previous editions.

The Developing Child

The normal state for the newborn child is complete dependence on its mother for all its wants: food, warmth, security, affection and hygiene. However, from the moment of birth the baby normally becomes increasingly aware of its surroundings and independent of its mother. The more important of the stages by which independence is reached are known as the 'milestones' of development. All children do not develop at the same rate, but it is possible to quote an average age for attainment of each milestone. As a general rule, boys tend to lag behind girls in all aspects of development.

A newly born baby shows a number of primitive reflexes, e.g. the 'placing' reflex, in which the foot is bent upwards and raised when the front of the leg is placed against the edge of a hard object; the 'walking' reflex, in which the legs are flexed and then extended when the baby is held with the soles of its feet on something solid; the 'grasp' reflex, in which the fingers or toes close into a grip when the palm or sole is stroked; the 'Moro' reflex, in which the baby shoots out its arms and opens its hands as if trying to save itself from falling, and then closes its arms together, when support is suddenly removed from behind its head; the 'rooting' reflex, in which the baby searches with its mouth for the nipple when its cheek comes in contact with its mother's breast. The walking reflex is normally lost by the end of the 1st month and the other reflexes by about the 4th month, as myelinization of the central nervous system proceeds. Other important reflexes concern the bowels and bladder, which empty automatically without respect for time, place or person.

By about the age of 4 months the average baby can hold its head off the pillow, and by between the 5th and 7th month its eye movements are co-ordinated so that it can follow an object without squinting. By about the 7th month it can sit unaided, by about 12 months it can stand and by about 18 months it can walk.

By the end of 12 months the average child can pick up small objects between the tips of the first finger and thumb. Its manual co-ordination improves, so that by the age of 18 months it can carry food successfully to its mouth with a spoon. By this age, too, the child is beginning to prefer to use one hand to the other. It normally has control of its bowels, and by the age of 2 years of its bladder also, although this latter control may be disturbed, particularly at night, until a much later age owing to emotional stresses.

Other motor skills gradually develop, so that at 3 years the average child can feed itself with a spoon and fork and can copy drawings of simple shapes, but not draw them from memory. By the age of 5 years the average child can wash, dress and undress itself, and can use a knife, fork and spoon skilfully.

One of the most important milestones is the development of language. Understanding of spoken words precedes a child's own use of words. Thus at 12 months a child is learning to obey commands and to understand the meaning of 'no'. Its own vocabulary is restricted to one or two meaningful words. The understanding of words and phrases increases rapidly between 1 and 2 years. The use of words advances less rapidly, the difference being more marked in boys than girls. However, by the age of 2 years the average child has a vocabulary of several hundred words, which it can use to form short sentences to express its wants and feelings and by the age of 5 years its vocabulary has grown to 2000 words. With increased vocabulary and understanding develops, ultimately, the ability to form abstract concepts such as morality and loyalty, understanding of which is essential before the child can take its full place in society.

Piaget's Concepts

Piaget claims that a child's intellectual development proceeds in the following stages, in which different kinds of thinking always succeed one another in the same order:

1. *Sensory-motor Stage*

During this stage the child is concerned only with objects it can directly perceive and it gains experience of them by handling and manipulating them. This stage normally ends at the age of about 18 months and is followed by the pre-conceptual stage.

2. *Pre-conceptual Stage*

During this stage the child is developing its ability to respond to objects in their absence, i.e. that it cannot directly perceive, as, for example, when it searches for a lost toy. It is developing its memory images, its powers of imaginative play and of language.

3. *Intuitive Thinking Stage*

During this stage, which normally begins at the age of about 4 years, the child's thinking is once again dominated by what it actually sees in front of it, and it makes no attempt to relate it to previous events. As a result it cannot, for example, understand that the total quantity of a fluid has remained the same when it has seen it poured from a glass container of one shape into another of obviously different shape and size. This stage normally lasts until the age of 7 years and is followed by the concrete operational thinking stage.

4. *Concrete Operational Thinking Stage*
During this stage the child begins to relate events to those that have preceded them and to those that follow and can, therefore, understand numbers as a series. It is able also to take account of two factors at once and of other viewpoints apart from its own.

5. *Abstract Operational Stage*
During this final stage of intellectual development, which normally begins at the age of about 11 years, the child begins to reason on the conceptual level.

There is some disagreement amongst psychologists as to the validity of Piaget's concept of stages of intellectual development, but it is being found useful in assessing the abilities of mentally handicapped children and in planning more helpful and realistic teaching and training programmes for them.

In the early months of life the child's emotional life is centred entirely around its mother, who satisfies all its needs. At this stage the child is unaware of any separate existence, but has started to become aware of its existence as a separate individual by the time it is 2 years old. This awareness is normally complete by the age of 3 years. Although at this age the child is becoming more and more aware of reality, fantasy still plays a considerable part in its life for the next 2 years. At this stage, too, irrational fears and night terrors are at their peak.

The child's immediate horizon widens to include, first, the father and other members of the family, and then individuals and groups outside its own family. The speed and extent to which this occurs depend on the parents' handling of this stage. At first, the child sees other children as rivals for its mother's affection and tends to revert to more infantile levels of behaviour in search of reassurance from its mother. The wise parent, while providing a consistent background of encouragement and security and affection, will not overprotect the child from environmental stresses, but will teach it to face them and adapt itself to them if they cannot be overcome. In this way the child's emotional development keeps pace with its intellectual development. However, parental mishandling at this stage, whether in the direction of over-protection or a too sudden severing of parental and emotional ties, may distort emotional development and result in immaturity of personality and neurotic traits in later life, including the inability to form satisfactory emotional relationships with members of the opposite sex.

By the time the normal child is 15 years old the basic potentiality for

5

independent existence is established, although the personality is at this stage still immature and continues to develop at varying rates and to varying degrees of maturity. From the interaction of intelligence, personality and environment evolves character—an individual's apparent ability to control and direct all his activities and desires.

In the case of the mentally handicapped there is delay in reaching, and in the case of the severely mentally handicapped, failure to reach, these various stages of development and integration, as a result of which the majority of the latter class are permanently incapable of leading an independent existence, in spite of treatment and training.

The Diagnosis of Mental Handicap

The diagnosis of mental handicap, although ultimately a psychiatric responsibility, is one to which parents, general practitioners, paediatricians, school teachers, nurses and school medical officers, occupational therapists, psychologists and social workers all contribute. Recent years have seen the establishment of assessment clinics, often as joint enterprises of Regional Hospital Boards and Local Health Authorities, to which suspected cases of mental handicap may be referred for diagnosis and advice concerning treatment and training. Where there is any doubt the patient is admitted temporarily to hospital for fuller investigation. There is no doubt that these clinics are much appreciated by parents and others responsible for the care of the mentally handicapped, and as they have become established, general practitioners are increasingly referring patients to them as they do to the out-patient clinics of other specialties.

The diagnosis of mental handicap is rarely possible and, with few exceptions, unwise in the first 6 months of life. The most important exception is Down's syndrome. When the suspicions aroused at birth by the characteristic facial appearance and other physical features of this condition are confirmed by chromosome analysis, the ultimate presence of some degree of severe mental handicap can be forecast with certainty. However, it is unwise at this stage to make a more precise estimate of the probable degree of mental handicap as this can vary greatly within the severely mentally handicapped range. The time and manner in which the parents' attention is drawn to their child's abnormality must be most carefully chosen, with due regard to the personality, stability and intelligence of them both. It is important that this should be done by someone with sufficient knowledge to give authoritative yet gentle answers to the inevitable questions which follow, and that the informing of the parents should not be delayed too long, lest they are previously brought face to face with the problem by ill-informed and callous acquaintances.

Mental handicap manifests itself in the developing child as retardation in attaining the various stages of development towards independence previously described, e.g. by a failure at 6 months of age to respond to its mother's smiles and caresses or to look about and show interest in its surroundings or to make any attempt to sit up or to grasp objects with its

7

hands as a normal child would do. Between the ages of 2 and 3 years the child is developing rapidly and it is during this period that the developmental delays in the mentally handicapped may first become obvious. The presence of mental handicap can be suspected if the milestones are consistently delayed by a third or more of the age at which they are normally present, e.g. if the child cannot walk by the age of 2 years or say a short sentence by the age of about 3 years, provided purely physical causes have been excluded in each case. It cannot be stressed too strongly, however, that these are merely grounds for suspecting the presence of mental handicap. The confirmation of the presence of this condition is a skilled task involving a complete assessment of all aspects of development, both physical and mental, with due allowance for adverse environmental influences. However, the author believes that, where parents press for definite diagnosis and prognosis, controlled pessimism is less harmful in the long run than unreasoned optimism, with its inevitable disappointments.

Severe mental handicap, not previously detected, quickly manifests itself when schooling begins as an obvious inability to keep pace with other children, and the child's sense of frustration in this respect may be expressed in behaviour disorders which were not previously present. Inquiry will usually reveal the same delayed development in preschool days described above.

In the least severe degrees of mental handicap the academic disturbance is much less obvious and the child may complete its schooling and go into the outside world before definite evidence of mental handicap occurs in the form of social inefficiency and irresponsibility—there is inability to keep any job for longer than a few weeks or jobs are frequently changed for trivial and inadequate reasons; late hours are kept, often in undesirable company, and parental guidance ignored. It is in individuals of this type that the most complete assessment of the previous history and of the present condition, both mental and physical, is required before a definite diagnosis of mental handicap is made.

Some cases of mental handicap do not come to light until the individual is brought before the court on some, very often, relatively minor charge, or it may not become apparent until he is actually in prison, although this is uncommon nowadays with psychological examination of offenders a more general practice.

Once a diagnosis of mental handicap is made in a family, advice is often sought by the parents concerning the probability of the condition occurring in later children. In the past much of this advice has been ill-founded, and it is highly desirable that it should in future be given only after the most careful consideration of all the relevant aspects, if possible by a specialist in human genetics who is best equipped to give statistically accurate forecasts of the probabilities.

Parents should be helped to be honest, first with themselves and later with other people, about the true nature of their child's disability. Unfortunately, they are still sometimes encouraged by well-meaning, but misguided, persons to adopt all sorts of euphemisms to hide the true condition. The acceptance of the knowledge that one's own child is mentally handicapped is never easy and creates inevitable and understandable emotional stresses, but until parents can themselves learn to be honest about their children in this way it cannot reasonably be expected that the general public will learn to accept them without fear and prejudice.

The assessment of mental handicap should not be a once and for all exercise, as it has unfortunately been so often in the past, but should be a continuous process with periodic review by members of the multi-disciplinary team which made the original diagnosis.

The Causes of Mental Handicap

The condition underlying the various degrees of mental handicap is known as 'amentia'. Some cases of amentia are known to be due to a genetic abnormality in the child itself, determined at the moment of conception or during the subsequent stages of division of the fertilized ovum. Other cases, without a genetic abnormality, are due to environmental factors which interfere with the development of the brain during pregnancy, during birth or at any other stage in the child's life before the genetically determined limits of its intelligence have been reached, usually about the age of 15 or 16 years. Some cases of amentia arise from a combination of both genetic and environmental factors, as, for example, in 'subcultural' amentia. It must be stressed, however, that even with the most careful exploration of family histories of the mentally handicapped and most careful examination of the individual's own history, it is often not possible in our present state of knowledge to decide with certainty the causation of all cases. This is, in part, a reflection on the inaccuracy of our present microscopical and biochemical techniques, and it seems highly probable that improved and new techniques will elucidate the causation of many of these at present unclassified cases of amentia in due course.

THE GENETIC BASIS OF INHERITANCE

The innumerable factors, known as 'genes', which determine the potential limits of the physical and mental characteristics of each individual, are carried in the fertilized female sex cell (ovum) by pairs of bodies, known as 'chromosomes', half of which are derived from the male and half from the female parent. Twenty-two of the pairs are called 'autosomal' and the other pair 'sex' chromosomes—either two X chromosomes in females or one X and one Y chromosome in males.

Chromosomes may be cultured from white blood cells and skin fibroblasts. Staining the cultured chromosomes with Giemsa dye, quinacrine mustard or acridine orange reveals fluorescent banding patterns which are specific for different chromosomes and provide a positive means of identifying them. It is then possible to arrange chromosomes in pairs, each with a similar banding pattern, and to number the autosomal chromosome pairs from 1 to 22, in decreasing order of size, plus a pair of sex chromosomes, making a normal total chromosome count of 46.

In an alternative method of classification, chromosome pairs are identified as follows: pairs 1 to 3, Group A; pairs 4 and 5, Group B; pairs 6 to 12, Group C; pairs 13 to 15, Group D; pairs 16 to 18, Group E; pairs 19 and 20, Group F; and pairs 21 and 22, Group G, plus one pair of sex chromosomes.

Whereas individual chromosomes can be seen under the microscope, the presence or absence of a particular gene can only be inferred from the effects produced.

The genes for some characteristics are capable of over-riding the effects of the corresponding genes derived from the other parent—such genes are said to be 'dominant' with respect to the other genes, which are called 'recessive'. A recessive gene can express itself only when another recessive gene for the same characteristic is inherited from the other parent. However, since both parents normally carry at least one pair of genes for each characteristic, but contribute only one gene of each pair to the fertilized ovum, it will be seen from the following diagram that the chance of both recessive genes coming together is only 1 in 4 and that in the other 3 cases the effects of the dominant gene will be produced.

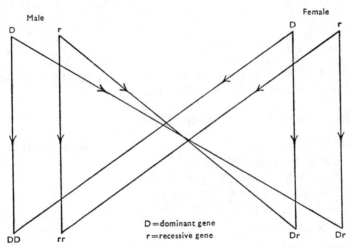

D = dominant gene
r = recessive gene

The genes which cause some cases of mental handicap are carried on the sex chromosomes and are referred to as 'sex-linked'. The following diagram indicates how a sex-linked abnormality may be transmitted to male offspring by female carriers who themselves escape, as do their female children. This is because the responsible gene, which is carried on

11

one of the X chromosomes, is recessive to the corresponding normal gene on the other X chromosome of the female chromosome pair, but is able to act unopposed in the male, in whom the second X chromosome is absent. However, in the rare event of an affected male marrying a female carrier there is a theoretical risk of half of any female as well as male offspring being affected.

This very brief account of some of the principles of human genetics is included merely as an introduction to a most complex subject and in order to explain terms used later in this book.

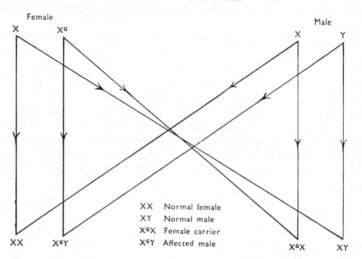

CLASSIFICATION OF CAUSES OF MENTAL HANDICAP WITH EXAMPLES OF SYNDROMES

CHROMOSOMAL ABNORMALITIES

Autosomes   *Mode of Inheritance*

    Cri du Chat (partial deletion 5)
    Down's Syndrome (Trisomy 21–22)
    Edwards' Syndrome (Trisomy 17–18)
    Patau's Syndrome (Trisomy 13–15)

Sex Chromosomes

    Fragile X Syndrome
    Trisomy X (XXX Syndrome)
    Trisomy XY (XXY, Klinefelter's
      Syndrome)
    Turner's Syndrome (XO)
    XYY Syndrome

Genetic

Ataxia Telangiectasia (Louis–Bar
    Syndrome)
Hypertelorism (Greig's Syndrome)
Laurence–Moon–Biedl Syndrome
Marinesco–Sjögren Syndrome   } Recessive
Microcephaly
Rud's Syndrome
Smith–Lemli–Opitz Syndrome
Virchow–Seckel–Dwarf
Acrocephalo–syndactyly (Apert's
    Syndrome)
Craniofacial Dysostosis (Crouzon's
    Syndrome)   } Dominant of poor
Mandibulofacial Dysostosis (Treacher   penetrance
    Collins or Berry–Franchescetti
    Syndrome)
Mandibulo–oculo–facial Dyscephaly   Dominant
    (Hallerman–Streiff Syndrome)
Tuberous sclerosis (Epiloia)   Dominant of variable
                                        penetrance or
                                        mutation

Albright's Syndrome
de Lange Syndrome
Prader–Willi Syndrome   } Unknown
Rubinstein–Taybi's Syndrome
Sturge–Weber Syndrome

INBORN ERRORS OF METABOLISM

Disorders of Protein Metabolism

Hartnup Disease
Histidinaemia
Homocystinuria   } Recessive
Maple Syrup Urine Disease
Phenylketonuria
Hyperuricaemia (Lesch–Nyhan   X-linked
    Syndrome

Disorders of Lipid Metabolism

Amaurotic Familial Idiocy
    (Cerebromacular Degeneration)   } Recessive
Gaucher's Disease
Niemann–Pick Disease

Disorders of Carbohydrate Metabolism

Galactosaemia   Recessive

Disorders of Connective Tissue Metabolism

Gargoylism (Hunter–Hurler
   Syndrome   X-linked/Recessive

Disorders of Mineral or Electrolyte Metabolism

Diabetes Insipidus (Nephrogenic)   Recessive
G–6–P–D Deficiency
Wilson's Disease   } X-linked

Other X-linked Disorders

Oculocerebral Degeneration
   (Norrie's Disease)
Renpenning's Syndrome (Some of these
   may now be cases of Fragile X Syndrome)
X-linked Hydrocephalus
X-linked Spastic Paraplegia

Endocrine Disorders

Hypothyroidism (Cretinism)

INFECTIONS

Ante-natal

   Cytomegalovirus
   Rubella
   Syphilis
   Toxoplasmosis
   Varicella

Post-natal

   Gastro-enteritis and Dehydration
   Meningitis
   Virus Encephalitis

ENVIRONMENTAL

Ante-natal

   Alcohol
   Radiation
   Rhesus Factor Incompatibility
   Teratogenic Substances

Anoxia
Gross Deprivation
Lead
Trauma

CHROMOSOMAL ABNORMALITIES

Since 1959, a number of chromosomal abnormalities have been consistently demonstrated in various syndromes associated with amentia. These abnormalities have included the presence of extra whole autosomal and sex chromosomes, and the 'deletion' or absence of parts of chromosomes, resulting in an excess or diminution, respectively, of the genes normally carried on those chromosomes.

The presence of an extra chromosome with a banding pattern identical to that of a chromosome pair is known as a 'trisomy'. This arises from the failure of members of that particular pair of chromosomes to separate (non-disjunction) during the early stages of division of the mother's sex cells (meiosis) and results in a chromosome count of 47 after fertilization, instead of the normal 46.

Sometimes, usually during meiosis, one member from each of two different autosomal pairs may become attached together to produce a compound chromosome. This process is known as 'translocation' and results in an apparent total chromosome count of 45 instead of the normal 46, but as there is almost no diminution in the total normal gene complement, no physical or intellectual abnormality results. However, as will be seen later, translocations may in some cases be transmitted to offspring and result in both physical and intellectual abnormalities.

The absence of a whole autosomal chromosome from any pair appears to be a lethal condition, but the absence of one of the sex chromosomes is not incompatible with life, although it is associated with physical abnormalities and, in some cases, with impaired intelligence. It has been claimed that the physical effects of an excess of genes are exactly the opposite of those of a diminution of the same genes—the 'mirror-image theory'.

Less consistently reported chromosomal abnormalities in other syndromes in amentia include 'constrictions' in the body of the chromosomes, 'ring forms', in which the ends of a partially deleted chromosome become joined together, the presence of 'satellites' or small fragments attached to chromosomes, and 'interstitial translocations' in which part of one chromosome becomes incorporated in the corresponding part of another.

As a result of abnormal separation of chromosomes during the later stages of cell division (mitosis), chromosome 'mosaics' may occur in

15

which a number of cells of the body contain an excess of chromosomes and the remainder a corresponding deficit.

AMNIOCENTESIS

It is now possible to detect most autosomal and sex chromosome abnormalities during pregnancy by culturing chromosomes from a small quantity of amniotic fluid drawn off from the uterus at about the 14th week of pregnancy. This enables the mother to be offered the opportunity of termination of pregnancy where abnormalities are revealed.

ULTRASOUND

Ultrasound is a useful non invasive technique used to detect fetal abnormalities with a structural defect such as spina bifida and microcephaly.

CHORION BIOPSY AND FETOSCOPY

Recently, newer techniques such as fetoscopy and chorion biopsy have been introduced. Chorion biopsy can be performed between the 6th and 10th week of pregnancy, and this means that some abnormalities can be diagnosed much earlier than by amniocentesis. In fetoscopy, blood samples from the fetus are taken from the umbilical cord and the technique may even be used to take fetal biopsies, for example of liver, making a more precise diagnosis possible.

DERMATOGLYPHICS

The increasing knowledge of significant chromosomal abnormalities has led to a renewed interest in finger-print and palm-print patterns, known as dermatoglyphics, and to an attempt to correlate specific patterns with specific chromosomal abnormalities. There are three basic finger-tip patterns: the 'whorl', the 'arch' and the 'loop'. Loops are referred to as 'radial' or 'ulnar' according to the direction in which they open. The density of the ridge systems, which make up these patterns, can be expressed numerically as the total ridge count for all ten fingers.

The palmar pattern is similarly made up of a number of ridge systems. The point where three ridge systems meet is known as a 'triradius'.

Particular attention is paid in dermatoglyphics to the relative incidence of the different types of finger-tip patterns, to the total ridge count and to the angle ('atd' angle) formed between the triradius at the base of the index finger (a), the most distal axial triradius on the palm of the hand (t), and the triradius at the base of the little finger (d). The normal 'atd' angle is about 48°.

16

CASES OF AMENTIA WITH KNOWN GENETIC ABNORMALITIES

A. AFFECTING CHROMOSOMES

The presence of extra, large chromosomes appears to be incompatible with life and may be found in fetuses which abort spontaneously. It is not until the thirteenth to fifteenth chromosomal pairs are reached that a fetus with an extra chromosome ('trisomy') becomes viable, but even then it has gross physical abnormalities and short expectation of life.

AUTOSOMAL TRISOMIES

1. Trisomy 13–15, Group D Trisomy (Patau's Syndrome)

The incidence of this trisomy is about 0·1 per 1000 live births and is related to advancing maternal age. The risk of recurrence is low unless either parent is a translocation carrier. The most commonly reported features are a small head and receding chin, various eye defects, low-set deformed ears, hare-lip and cleft palate and polydactyly (extra fingers and toes). There are specific abnormalities in the brain and congenital heart abnormalities may be present. Dermatoglyphics show an increase in the frequency of radial loops in the finger-tip patterns and there is often a single transverse palmar crease ('simian crease'). The 't' triradius is very distally placed, resulting in a very wide 'atd' angle of over 100°. A proximally placed tibial loop is commonly found on the hallucal area of the sole of the foot.

The degree of mental handicap is severe and it is rare for infants with Patau's syndrome to live for more than 6 months.

2. Trisomy 17–18, Group E Trisomy (Edwards' Syndrome)

The incidence of this trisomy is about 0·5 per 1000 live births and is related to advancing maternal age. It occurs about twice as frequently in females as in males. The risk of recurrence is small unless either parent is a translocation carrier. The features of trisomy 17–18 overlap to a considerable degree those of trisomy 13–15. However, the most commonly reported features of trisomy 17–18 are anteroposterior elongation of the skull, receding chin, low-set deformed ears, webbing of the neck, congenital heart defects, fingers which are flexed and tend to overlap, retroflexible and distally placed thumbs, limited hip abduction, 'rocker bottom' feet, short, dorsiflexed big toes and spasticity. The toenails are often hypoplastic. In the brain the frontal lobes of the cerebral hemispheres fail to separate normally.

Dermatoglyphics show a striking preponderance of arches in the finger-tip patterns, forming over 80 per cent of all patterns in infants with this syndrome. The 't' triradius may be distally displaced, but less so than in trisomy 13–15. As in Patau's syndrome, the degree of mental handicap in Edwards' Syndrome is severe and affected infants have a poor sucking reflex and rarely live for more than 6 months. However, a case of apparent trisomy 18 has been reported in a girl of nearly 9 years who was severely mentally handicapped, with a small, round head, low hairline on the neck, shallow orbits, deformed ears, beaked nose, small mouth, high arched palate and underdeveloped teeth, scoliosis, shield-like chest with underdeveloped nipples, heart murmur, small external genitalia, flexion contractures of the arms and fingers with ulnar deviation and bilateral simian creases, and flexion contractures of the legs with bilateral club feet.

Dermatoglyphics showed hypoplastic dermal ridges, with arches on all the finger tips of both hands.

3. Trisomy 21, Group G Trisomy (Down's Syndrome; Mongolism)

Trisomy 21 is, in fact, a misnomer. When the presence of an extra small acrocentric chromosome was discovered in Down's syndrome in 1959 it was thought to be identical to members of pair 21. However, the fluorescent banding patterns of the extra chromosome are those of pair 22. Down's syndrome should, therefore, be correctly called trisomy 22, but to avoid confusion, it has been decided by international agreement to continue to refer to Down's syndrome as trisomy 21.

In about 4–5 per cent of cases of Down's syndrome, the extra chromosome has become attached to a member of another pair of chromosomes to produce a 13/21, 15/21, 21/21 or 21/22 translocation. The resulting compound chromosome has the appearance of a single chromosome, so that the total chromosome count appears to be 46 instead of the 47 expected in any trisomic condition. Either parent may be the carrier of such a translocation and will have an apparent total chromosome count of only 45. In some cases of Down's syndrome the total chromosome count is higher than 47 due to the presence of one or more extra female X chromosomes, which are accompanied by various abnormalities of sexual development.

The overall incidence of Down's syndrome is 1·8 per 1000 (1 in 600) live births, but the incidence ranges from about 1 in 2000 live births at the lower end of the child-bearing period to about 1 in 50 live births at the end of that period. Down's syndrome occurs in most races and cases have been reported in Chinese, Japanese and Negroes. Parents frequently avoid having any more children after the birth of a child with Down's syndrome, so that the child's most common position in the family is either first (and only) or last, but up to 5 cases among siblings have been reported, as well as identical twins with Down's syndrome and twins in which one had Down's syndrome and the other was quite normal.

The cause of the non-disjunction resulting in the trisomic condition in

Down's syndrome (whether translocated or not) cannot, as yet, be stated categorically, but a number of relevant facts are known.

Cases of Down's syndrome may be divided into two groups: one in which the incidence is independent of the maternal age at the time of conception and the other in which it is dependent on that factor. The first group is numerically smaller than the second and contains both trisomic and translocation cases, the latter being in the minority. In some of these cases the translocation is transmitted by a parent and in others arises sporadically. A proportion of cases are born to mothers who are, in fact, themselves Down's syndrome mosaics.

As already stated, the incidence of Down's syndrome increases with advancing maternal age at the time of conception, but the reason for this is not yet known. Virus infection (particularly infectious hepatitis) in the mother, or immunization of the mother with live viruses, maternal exposure to radiation, either diagnostic or random, increased maternal thyroid antibodies, lowered urinary oestriol excretion during pregnancy and altered pH of the blood, have all been suggested as possibly significant aetiological factors in Down's syndrome. However, none has, as yet, received general acceptance, but it is possible that the chromosomal abnormalities in Down's syndrome may be brought about by a wide variety of different factors, including those just mentioned.

Clinical Features

Babies with Down's syndrome are often born before their expected date of delivery with a low birth weight. The typical features of Down's syndrome are present at birth. Facially they bear a strong resemblance to each other. The skull is brachycephalic due to the failure of its basal segments to elongate normally. As a result, the head in Down's syndrome is small and round, the transverse and anteroposterior diameters are almost the same and the back of the skull is flattened. The hair on the scalp does not, in the authors' experience, differ as much in texture from the normal as is often suggested. However, the beard and axillary hair are scanty and the pubic hair is straight. The palpebral fissures slope downwards and inwards and often the upper eyelid overlaps the lower at the inner canthus, the so-called 'epicanthic fold'. Various abnormalities in the eye themselves occur. Very frequently there is a fine white speckling of the iris known as 'Brushfield spots'. Cataracts may be present, as may be strabismus or nystagmus. The nose is small, with a poorly developed bridge which makes the eyes look farther apart than normal, whereas the opposite is, in fact, the case. The ears are small, of simple pattern, and often with poorly developed lobes. The palate is high, arched and short and the tongue tends to protrude, although it is not usually much larger than normal. It shows various degrees of transverse furrowing. The teeth develop late and may be abnormal in their size, shape and alignment.

The neck is short and thick, so that sometimes the head appears to be set directly on the shoulders. The limbs are shorter than normal and, even when fully grown, people with Down's syndrome are well below normal height. The pelvis shows constant variations from the normal, which produce a diagnostic appearance on X-ray examination. The muscles generally are hypotonic, enabling joints to be hyper-extended and strange postures to be adopted. The abdomen is protuberant and an umbilical hernia may be present.

Next to the facial appearance the hands are the most typical feature of Down's syndrome: the palm is square and a transverse palmar crease ('four-finger line' or simian crease) occurs in between 30 and 40 per cent of cases; the fingers, which may be webbed (syndactyly), are shorter than normal, particularly the fifth finger, which may not extend beyond the first interphalangeal joint of the fourth finger. In over 50 per cent of cases it may be incurving (clinodactyly), with only a single flexion crease in about 15 per cent of cases. The thumb, too, is shorter than normal and may extend only to the metacarpophalangeal joint of the index finger.

The great toe, also, is shorter than normal and is separated from the second toe by a wide gap which may extend as a cleft onto the sole of the foot. Syndactyly of the toes may be present. The dermatoglyphic pattern of the hands and feet in Down's syndrome are pathognomonic and may enable a diagnosis to be made in doubtful cases before a chromosome analysis can be completed. In Down's syndrome the most distal triradius is near the centre of the palm, so that the 'atd' angle (about 80°) is almost twice the normal. The finger-tip patterns show fewer whorls and arches than in the general population. The number of radial loops is reduced and the number of ulnar loops increased, occurring on all 10 fingers in over 30 per cent of cases of Down's syndrome. Where radial loops are present in Down's syndrome they are typically on one or both ring fingers. The typical palm print shows a large hypothenar pattern, a very small or absent thenar pattern and a digital loop between the bases of the third and fourth fingers. Another typical feature is the absence of any pattern on the hallucal area of the sole in about 50 per cent of cases of Down's syndrome.

Congenital cardiac abnormalities are far less commonly present in adults with Down's syndrome than is usually believed, possibly because they have caused death at an early age—slightly over 50 per cent of all children with Down's syndrome die during the first year of life. However, peripheral circulatory disturbances are common and in cold weather the lips, hands and feet are often cyanosed and chilblains occur. Congenital abnormalities of other internal organs may also be present such as atresia of the upper part of the gastro-intestinal tract. Hirschsprung's disease (congenital dilatation of the colon) frequently occurs in Down's syndrome. The brain in Down's syndrome is smaller than normal with simplification of the gyral pattern.

People with Down's syndrome are characteristically mouth breathers and are very prone to severe respiratory infections, which previously caused their early death, but with the introduction of antibiotics their expectation of life has increased considerably. At the beginning of the century it was rare for anyone with Down's syndrome to survive in hospital beyond his 10th birthday. Now the average age of death of such a patient is approaching 60 years. Patients with Down's syndrome cared for in hospitals appear to be more susceptible to infections than other groups, although the increased susceptibility seems to be greater in males than females. However, both sexes are very prone to chronic blepharitis, due to the absence from the tears of the enzyme lysozyme, which normally prevents infection. Some 10 per cent of Down's syndrome patients are found to have been infected with viral hepatitis without necessarily having shown clinical signs of jaundice themselves. Of these some are carriers but only a few remain highly infectious, the disease being transmitted in the blood or secretions. Lymphocytic thyroiditis occurs in about 30 per cent of cases of Down's syndrome, affecting females more frequently than males.

Epilepsy and cerebral palsy are rare accompaniments of Down's syndrome, possibly because the brachycephalic skull undergoes relatively little moulding during labour, with consequently reduced risk of brain damage due to abnormal compression.

It has been believed for some years that children with Down's syndrome run twenty times the random risk of developing acute leukaemia, but it has recently been suggested that transient leukaemoid reactions which are rare in normal children may, in the past, have been mistaken for true leukaemia in children with Down's syndrome and that the incidence of true leukaemia may be the same in both types of children.

The mean red cell volume has been shown to be abnormally increased in many non-anaemic patients with Down's syndrome, but the significance of this finding is not at present understood. A large number of studies of erythrocyte enzymes in Down's syndrome have been carried out with conflicting results.

People with Down's syndrome vary widely in their degree of mental incapacity within a wide range of IQ and achievements, including, in some cases, the ability to read and write, but all chromosomally confirmed cases fall within the severely handicapped category judged on the criterion of their inability to lead an independent existence. Their practical ability exceeds their reasoning ability. Most sit by the age of 1 year and learn to walk between the ages of 2 and 3 years. They have an outstanding capacity for mimicry (in which they are no respecters of persons!) and it is this which makes them appear brighter intellectually than in fact they are. They are affectionate and characteristically cheerful, and, although often mischievous, as a group are the most easily managed of all ambulant mentally handicapped patients. They are musical and have a strongly developed sense of rhythm. In spite of their superficial similarity as regards physical appearance and temperamental characteristics, they show many personal variations and should therefore always be treated as individuals.

The libido is very much reduced in Down's syndrome. There is no record of a male with Down's syndrome fathering a child and there are only 13 published cases of females with Down's syndrome giving birth. In only 5 cases did the child itself suffer from the same condition. Evidence suggests that it is only the translocation type of Down's syndrome which is transmissible to the child.

People with Down's syndrome show senile degenerative brain changes with associated dementia at an earlier age than the rest of the population. This means that it is particularly important for them to have adequate training and education while they are young and their capacity to retain new information is at its best. The dementia which occurs in Down's syndrome is of an Alzheimer's type and it has been found that families which have individuals suffering from Alzheimer's dementia also have a higher than average incidence of members with Down's syndrome. The reason for this link is not yet known.

Some mentally handicapped people show only partial features of Down's syndrome and are usually of more normal stature and higher intelligence. Such people are best described as 'mongoloid'. They frequently show the mosaic pattern on chromosome analysis, with the extra 21 chromosomes present in only half the body's cells and with dermatoglyphic patterns intermediate between those of true trisomy 21 and the normal.

Genetic Counselling

The risk to parents who have already had a child with regular trisomy 21 of having another child similarly affected is about 1 in 100, irrespective of the age of the mother. However, the risk is greatly increased if either parent is the carrier of a translocated 21 chromosome, e.g. in the case of 15/21 translocation the risk is about 1 in 10 where the mother is the carrier, and about 1 in 20 where the father is the carrier. In the case of 21/22 translocation the risks are slightly higher, about 1 in 6 where the mother is the carrier, and about 1 in 12 where the father is the carrier. However, where either the mother or the father is the carrier of the fortunately rare 21/21 translocation, all their children will have Down's syndrome. Advancing paternal age at the time of conception appears to be a significant factor in the 21/22 translocation group.

It has recently been suggested that one-third to one-half the mothers with more than one child with Down's syndrome are themselves Down's mosaics. However, genetically transmitted forms of Down's syndrome appear, on present evidence, to account for less than 2 per cent of all cases so that the prevention of such cases would have little effect on the prevalence of this condition. On the other hand, the incidence of Down's syndrome could be reduced by a half by the detection by amniocentesis and subsequent termination of pregnancy in all positive cases in women aged 35 and over.

OTHER AUTOSOMAL CHROMOSOMAL ABNORMALITIES

Partial Trisomies

Mental handicap may be associated with the presence of extra chromosome material which can be identified as similar to that of part of a chromosome in the normal chromosome complement.

1. *Chromosome 4–5 Group B*

The presence of extended long arms in one member of a pair in the 4–5 chromosome group B has not yet been shown to produce a constant and specific physical syndrome, but the following abnormalities have been associated with it: reduced stature and weight, microcephaly, anti-mongoloid slope of the eyes, epicanthic folds, moderate ptosis, hypertelorism, beak-shaped nose, high narrow palate, widely spaced incisors and malshaped ears and narrow ear canals.

Dermatoglyphics have been reported as showing a simian crease, wide 'atd' angles and reduced ridge counts.

2. *Mosaic Trisomy 8*

Physical abnormalities reported in this condition include strabismus, large ears, everted lower lip, broad fingers with dystrophic finger nails, metatarsus–varus deformity and deep plantar creases.

Dermatoglyphics show the unusual presence of both arches and whorls on the finger tips and a whorl on the fourth interdigital area of the palm. The total finger ridge count is low and a simian crease may be present. The pattern intensity on the soles is high with an increase in the number of whorls, including the very rare type on the fourth interdigital area.

3. *Partial Trisomy 15*

Children with partial trisomy 15 are less severely handicapped physically and mentally than those with full trisomy 13–15 (Patau's syndrome). They are below normal in stature and weight. Physical abnormalities described include anti-mongoloid shape of the eyes, alternating strabismus, epicanthic folds, wide nasal bridge, large mouth with full lips and widely spaced teeth, large ears, mild thoracid kyphosis, valgus deformity of the elbow, and spindle-shaped fingers, with a short fifth finger.

Chromosome Deletions

1. *Chromosome 5—Deletion of Short Arm ('Cri du Chat' Syndrome)*

In this condition, which affects females more frequently than males, there is a partial deletion of the short arm of one of the fifth pair of chromosomes. Affected children usually have a low birth weight at maturity and subsequent growth is retarded. The facial appearance is not sufficiently specific to suggest the diagnosis—features most frequently reported are microcephaly, anti-mongoloid slope of the eyes, epicanthic folds, strabismus, a broad flattened nose with hypertelorism, low set ears and a small mouth. The main clue to the diagnosis is the characteristic cry of the newborn baby from which the syndrome derives its name; it is said to resemble the mewing cry of an injured kitten. This cry is believed to be associated with underdevelopment of the upper part of the larynx. The degree of mental handicap is severe.

As the child becomes older the typical cry disappears and other physical features appear, including dental malocclusion, short metacarpals and metatarsals, small wings of the iliac bones of the pelvis, flat feet, prematurely greying hair and increasing spasticity and exaggerated reflexes.

Dermatoglyphics show a slight excess of whorls with a corresponding decrease in the number of ulnar loops in the finger-print patterns. A pattern on the fourth interdigital area is a frequent occurrence, as is the presence of a simian crease and the absence of thenar and hypothenar patterns.

The incidence of the 'cri du chat' syndrome is unrelated to maternal age, and the risk of recurrence is low unless either of the parents is the carrier of a translocation in which the deleted portion of the short arm of chromosome number 5 is attached to another chromosome.

2. *Chromosome 4—Deletion of Short Arm (Wolf's Syndrome)*

There is a partial deletion of the short arm of one chromosome in pair 4. A number of the features of this syndrome are similar to those of the 'cri du chat' syndrome, e.g. low birth weight and retarded growth, microcephaly, anti-mongoloid slope of the eyes, epicanthic folds, strabismus, a broad flattened nose with hypertelorism and a small mouth. However, the typical cry does not occur in Wolf's syndrome, in which other common distinguishing physical features are coloboma of the iris, preauricular and sacral dimples, cleft palate, fish-shaped mouth, hypospadias and delayed bone maturation. The degree of mental handicap is more severe than that in the 'cri du chat' syndrome and seizures occur more frequently.

Dermatoglyphics show a lower ridge count than in the 'cri du chat' syndrome, with a higher frequency of arches on the finger tips, a higher frequency of double loops on the thumbs and a lower frequency of thenar and hypothenar patterns.

3. Chromosome 18—Partial Deletion of Long Arm

The deletion affects the long arm of one chromosome in pair 18. Children with this abnormality are small at birth and slow in their growth. They have small heads and a characteristic facial appearance. The middle part of the face is poorly developed, the eyes are deeply set and the bridge of the nose is underdeveloped. The chin, in contrast, is well developed. There is a typical deformity of the external ears, with overdevelopment of the helix, antihelix and antitragus. The muscular tone is generally poor. There is frequently a simian crease and the fingers and thumbs are usually long and tapering.

Dermatoglyphics show a high count of whorls on the fingers.

The degree of mental handicap is moderate.

There is some evidence of immunoglobulin deficiency in this condition.

4. Chromosome 21—Partial Deletion of Long Arm
('Antimongolism')

When first described it was claimed that this syndrome illustrated well the 'mirror-image' theory already referred to and it was so called because the physical features were said to be the opposite of those in mongolism (Down's syndrome). However, it now appears that those most frequently described do not support this claim—they include cataract, broad nasal bridge, low-set ears, inguinal hernia, hypospadias, scrotal dysplasia and club foot.

Ring Chromosomes

1. Chromosome Group 6–12, Group C

The presence of a ring chromosome in the chromosome group 6–12 has been reported in association with severe mental handicap accompanied by various physical abnormalities of the face and limbs, but so far no constant picture has emerged.

2. Chromosome Group 13–15, Group D ('Cat Eye' Syndrome)

It seems probable that the ring in this syndrome arises from chromosome 13 from partial deletions of both its short and long arms. In some cases only the long arms are affected without the formation of a ring. The most commonly reported features are severe mental handicap, microcephaly, coloboma of the iris, hypertelorism, malformed ears with preauricular skin tags or dimples, congenital heart disease, slender finger-like thumbs, clinodactyly of the fifth fingers, anal atresia, hypospadias, scrotal and perineal abnormalities in males and rectovaginal fistulae in females.

25

Dermatoglyphic reports have included the presence of ulnar loops on all the finger tips and radial arches in the hypothenar area, with absence of an axial triradius on both palms.

SEX CHROMOSOMAL ABNORMALITIES

The presence of extra X chromosomes carries with it the increased risk of mental handicap. In males, as a general rule, the greater the number of extra X chromosomes present the greater the physical deformity and the more severe the mental handicap. This suggests that the inactivation of all but one X chromosome is only partial and not complete as the 'Lyonization' hypothesis requires. In females the effect is less marked. On the other hand, the absence of an X chromosome is not incompatible with normal intelligence. Thus, in Turner's syndrome with an XO complement, physical and sexual abnormalities occur, but mental handicap is rare.

The partially inactivated X chromosomes in each cell become tightly coiled and, on staining, appear as dark masses (Barr bodies or sex chromatin masses) beneath the nuclear membrane. There is always one less Barr body present than the number of X chromosomes present in the cell—thus a normal female has one Barr body and is said to be 'chromatin positive' and the normal male no Barr body and is said to be 'chromatin negative'. There is an inverse ratio between the number of X chromosomes present and the total ridge count in the dermatoglyphics.

A number of mental handicap syndromes are inherited in a sex-linked manner and when a pregnant woman is known to be a carrier of such a condition it is important for purposes of genetic counselling to determine the sex of the fetus. This may be done by staining cultured fetal fibroblast cells, obtained by amniocentesis, with quinacrine mustard, which produces distinctive fluorescent patterns by which Barr bodies and Y chromosomes can be distinguished with certainty in single pregnancies. However, in multiple pregnancies involving fetuses of different sexes, errors may occur unless cells are obtained from within each amniotic sac, located with the help of ultrasound. The abnormalities of the sex chromosomes associated with mental handicap may be divided into four main sub groups:

1. Trisomy X (XXX Syndrome)

This syndrome has an overall incidence of nearly 1 in 1000 female births. It is estimated to occur in up to 1 per cent of mentally handicapped females. Like other sex chromosomal abnormalities its incidence is independent of maternal age. It produces no obvious physical or sexual abnormality and is, therefore, not always recognized. The degree of mental handicap is slight. Affected women are usually fertile and give birth to normal children.

A number of cases with up to 2 extra X chromosomes have been reported, but cases with more than this are exceedingly rare and only 4 cases with 3 extra X chromosomes (Syndrome XXXXX) have so far been reported.

Women with the XXXXX syndrome are severely mentally handicapped, with numerous skeletal abnormalities, many of which occur also in the XXXXY syndrome in males. Such abnormalities include deformities of the elbow, involving the ulna in particular, deformities of the wrist, again involving the ulna, clinodactyly of the fifth finger and deformities of the pelvis and knees which, as a result, tend to be held in a flexed position when standing. In females the breasts are poorly developed, the pubic hair is scanty and the uterus small.

Dermatoglyphics have shown the presence of arches on all 10 finger tips in 1 case.

2. Trisomy XY (XXY, Klinefelter's Syndrome)

This is the commonest sex chromosome abnormality and occurs in about 1 in 500 males, but in slightly over 1 per cent of all mentally handicapped males, most frequently in the less severely handicapped. Because of the presence of an extra X chromosome such cases have a Barr body and are referred to as chromatin positive. Children with this abnormality develop normally until puberty when the male secondary characteristics fail to appear, and in their place female bodily proportions and gynaecomastia may develop.

Affected individuals achieve performance IQ's on intelligence testing which are consistently higher than their verbal IQ's.

Klinefelter's syndrome may be associated with Down's syndrome so that the chromosome constitution is trisomy 21 + XXY, giving a chromosome count of 48.

Less common, and progressively more severely mentally handicapped, are those males who have up to three extra X chromosomes (XXXXY syndrome).

Affected males tend to be tall, due to delayed union of the piphyses at the ends of the long bones, and they show many of the other skeletal abnormalities already discussed in the XXXXX syndrome. Their external genitalia and secondary sexual characteristics are underdeveloped.

As in XXXXX females dermatoglyphics show a low total ridge count and a preponderance of arches on the finger tips. The 'd' triradius has been found to be absent in some cases of the XXXXY syndrome.

3. XYY Syndrome

The latest surveys suggest that the incidence of this syndrome is about 1 in 700 males. It has also been reported in identical twins. Affected males are over 6 ft (183 cm) tall and are normal in their general physical and sexual development and do not transmit their chromosomal abnormality to their offspring. There is no consistent evidence of any hormonal abnormalities or of any connection between a variety of bone abnormalities which have been reported and the presence of the extra Y chromosome.

The first discovery of the XYY syndrome in the residents of the special hospitals for patients with criminal and antisocial tendencies understandably led to the suggestion of a causal relationship between the chromosomal abnormality and the behaviour disorder. However, it is now clear that there are a number of males with the XYY syndrome living in the community and showing none of these antisocial tendencies. The cases reported from special hospitals were mildly handicapped in intelligence, but there is so far no conclusive evidence that males with the XYY syndrome run a higher risk of having intelligence below the normal than unaffected males.

Recent surveys among patients with the XYY syndrome in special hospitals and forensic psychiatric clinics suggest that these patients have difficulties in making relationships and have few friends. They tend to be impulsive and hot-tempered and to be easily provoked into acts of violence because of their lack of self-control. However, their convictions have been more frequently for offences against property than against people and their criminal activities have often begun at a very young age. There is evidence that enlargement of the Y chromosome in males with an otherwise normal XY chromosome constitution may carry with it an increased risk of personality disorder and violent and criminal behaviour.

Some male patients have an extra X as well as an extra Y chromosome (XXYY syndrome). They show a similar tendency to violent behaviour but are characteristically more obviously mentally handicapped. Males with sex chromosome abnormalities in special hospitals have been reported as having a higher than expected prevalence of EEG abnormalities, which almost invariably involved the background activity with an increased frequency of slow wave activity.

4. Fragile X Syndrome

When blood is cultured in a folic-acid deficient medium, some cells of certain individuals will show an indentation close to the end of one of the long arms of an X chromosome. This is known as a fragile X chromosome. It is present in only a percentage of cells, but has been found to have significance as a marker for one form of familial mental handicap found mainly in males but also in some of the female carriers of the abnormal chromosome. The male subjects with the disorder show a number of characteristic physical features, the most constant being macro-orchidism. They tend to have similar faces, with prominent wide mandible, wide noses set in a long face and large ears. Some have strikingly pale-blue eyes. They usually suffer from moderate to severe mental handicap and may have specific speech difficulties.

Sex Chromosome Mosaics
About one-third of all chromatin-positive males are XY/XXY mosaics and a third or more of all females with additional X chromosomes are mosaics.

B. AFFECTING GENES

A number of syndromes associated with mental handicap show no gross chromosomal abnormalities, but are due to abnormal genes. Some of these syndromes can be recognized by the typical facial appearance. The most common is 'true' microcephaly.

'True' Microcephaly
The skull is usually said to be microcephalic when its circumference is less than 43 cm in an adult. Environmental factors during pregnancy may interfere with the development of the brain and skull and result in microcephaly. These factors will be referred to later. In the case of 'true' microcephaly, however, the condition is inherited in an autosomal recessive manner with an incidence of about 1 in 1000 live births, and several children in the same generation of a family may be effected.

The striking feature of this condition is not merely the smallness of the head, but rather the marked disproportion between the face of a normal size and the tiny cranial vault. In profile the appearance is characteristic, with a markedly receding chin and forehead. Sometimes the scalp has a corrugated appearance ('cutis verticis gyrata'), but this condition is not confined to microcephaly and its aetiology is unknown. It occurs mostly in males, in whom it develops slowly between the ages of 20 and 30 years. These patients are usually short in stature and may have various associated neurological abnormalities. A number suffer from epilepsy.

The majority are within the severely mentally handicapped range, although some may be mentally handicapped. They are usually pleasant in manner and well behaved.

Apart from its overall small size, the brain may show various developmental abnormalities: there may be a failure of development of the secondary gyri or the gyri may be very much narrower than normal ('microgyria') or there may be large cystlike spaces in the substance of the brain ('porencephaly').

Bird-Headed Dwarf (Virchow–Seckel–Dwarf)
This condition is inherited in an autosomal recessive manner.

Affected children are small for their gestational age and are of slender body build. They have a bird-like appearance due to microcephaly, prominent eyes, hypoplasia of the malar bones, a prominent, sometimes beaked nose and a receding chin. The ears are lowset, with absent lobes. The palate is high and arched and may be cleft. The teeth may be absent or atrophic and the enamel hypoplastic.

There may be skeletal abnormalities such as dislocation of the head of the radius and congenital dislocation of the hips, with wide spacing between the first and second toes.

Any degree of mental handicap may occur.

Acrocephalo-syndactyly (Apert's Syndrome)

This syndrome is inherited in an autosomal dominant manner, but the gene concerned has poor penetrance so that only partial features of the disease may occur.

The facial appearance is characteristic. The skull is oxycephalic, i.e. it is elongated upwards, hence the description 'tower skull' or 'steeple skull' sometimes applied. On X-ray examination the skull may be thinned and its inner table may show a 'copper-beaten' appearance. The eyes are markedly protuberant. The palate is high and narrow like a Gothic arch and the teeth are very irregular.

The facial appearance is due to the premature fusion of the bones in the base of the skull, so that the orbits are shallow and the brain, being unable to develop laterally, has to do so vertically, expanding the skull in the same direction.

There are gross abnormalities of the hands and feet. The fingers and toes may be entirely rudimentary or may be fused with adjacent fingers or toes.

The degree of mental handicap varies.

Craniofacial Dysostosis (Crouzon's Syndrome)

This syndrome is inherited in a similar manner to that of acrocephalo-syndactyly and produces a somewhat similar facial appearance and similar X-ray appearances of the skull. However, in contrast to that condition, limb abnormalities do not occur and mental handicap is present in only about 20 per cent of cases.

Hypertelorism (Greig's Syndrome)

This condition appears to be inherited in an autosomal recessive manner.

The condition is characterized by the typical facial appearance, in which the bridge of the nose is broad and flattened and the eyes are very widely set. This is due to overgrowth of that part of the sphenoid bone in the base of the skull which develops from cartilage. The palate is usually high and narrow, like a Gothic arch.

Hypertelorism, in which the distance between the eyes themselves is, in fact, greater than normal, has to be distinguished from 'telecanthus', in which the appearance is similar but in that case due to an increased distance between the inner canthi of the lids of the two eyes.

In some cases, the fingers and toes are similar to those in Down's syndrome and a connection has been suggested between the two conditions. Another feature common to both conditions is the incidence of congenital heart defects.

Mentally, those affected are usually within the severely mentally handicapped range, although on occasions they are classifiable as mentally handicapped and in rare cases, are of normal intelligence.

Hypertelorism may also occur as a feature of other genetically determined syndromes associated with mental handicap.

FIRST ARCH SYNDROMES

Mental handicap of varying degree occurs in several of the syndromes associated with abnormal development of the structures arising embryologically from the first branchial arch. There is a considerable overlap of the features of the various syndromes in this group:

1. Cervico-oculo-acoustic Dysplasia (Syndrome of Wildervanck)

The mode of inheritance of this syndrome is not known with certainty. The main features are perceptive nerve deafness and absence or delay in the development of speech, paralysis of the external rectus of one or both eyes, retractio bulbi and features of the Klippel–Feil syndrome (extreme shortness and limited movement of the neck, due to fusing of the cervical vertebrae, and a low hairline).

The intelligence may vary from normal to the severely mentally handicapped.

2. Mandibulo-facial Dyostosis (Treacher–Collins or Berry–Franchescetti Syndrome)

This syndrome is inherited in an autosomal dominant manner due to a gene of poor penetrance.

The face has a typical appearance, which has been variously described as bird-, fish- or sheep-like. This is due to gross under-development of the bones of the cheek and chin. The mouth is enlarged, the palate is high and there may be a cleft palate and hare-lip. The teeth are malformed.

The eyes have an anti-mongoloid shape. There is a notch ('coloboma') at the outer end of the lower eyelid.

The ears are malformed, with a narrow external auditory meatus and malformation of the middle and inner ear, resulting in deafness. There is a blind fistula between the angle of the mouth and the ear.

The hair grows forwards onto the cheek in a tongue-like process from above the ear.

31

The height and head circumference are below average.

The degree of mental handicap varies from the mild to the severe. The facial appearance and deafness often suggest a degree of mental handicap much more severe than is, in fact, the case, if the effects of the patient's isolation can be overcome by operation or by special training for the deaf.

3. Mandibulo-oculo-facial Dyscephaly (Hallerman–Streiff Syndrome)

This syndrome is inherited in an autosomal dominant manner.

The facial appearance is somewhat similar to that in mandibulo-facial dysotosis. As in the latter condition, the bones of the cheek and chin are underdeveloped, the palate is high and narrow and the teeth are malformed. In the present condition the nose is beaked and there is a double cutaneous chin with a central cleft.

The eyes are smaller than usual, and congenital cataracts, nystagmus and strabismus may be present.

The skin of the face is atrophic, particularly that of the nose. 'Alopecia areata' occurs in the scalp, eyebrows and eyelashes. The height and head circumference are below average.

The degree of mental handicap varies from mild to severe.

4. Rubinstein–Taybi's Syndrome

The evidence points to a genetic basis for this condition, although this is not yet proved.

The facial appearance is less abnormal than in the previously described first arch syndromes. The eyes have an anti-mongoloid slant, the nose is beaked and the palate high and narrow, but the bones of the cheek and chin are more normally developed. The ears are often of simple pattern and may be low-set or rotated. There may also be pigmented naevi of the forehead or sacrum and various skeletal abnormalities, but the feature by which the syndrome can be most easily recognized is the abnormal breadth of the thumbs and big toes.

The degree of mental handicap is usually severe.

Dermatoglyphics have a high incidence of dermal ridge patterns on the thenar and hallucal areas, with a large loop opening into the first interdigital area in the latter case.

5. Smith–Lemli–Opitz Syndrome

This condition is inherited in an autosomal recessive manner. Affected children have low birth weights, microcephaly and a characteristic facial appearance due to ptosis, a short nose with a flattened bridge and anteverted nostrils, and an underdeveloped chin. Cleft palate and cardiac abnormalities are frequently present. There are simian creases on the palms and syndactyly of the toes. Hypospadias and cryptorchidism occur in males.

The degree of mental handicap is usually severe but, on occasions, may be mild.

Dermatoglyphics show a high number of digital whorls and a reduced frequency of ulnar loops.

OTHER SYNDROMES OF GENETIC ORIGIN

In the following syndromes of genetic origin the facial appearance is less abnormal than in those previously described.

1. Ataxia Telangiectasia (Louis–Bar Syndrome)

This condition is inherited in an autosomal recessive manner.

Affected children appear normal at birth, but between the ages of 3 and 5 years develop 'telangiectasia' (prominent dilated capillaries) on the conjunctiva of the eyeball, spreading to the eyelids, the face, ears and neck, the antecubital fossa, the wrists and hands, the popliteal fossa and sometimes the feet. There may also be *café-au-lait* spots and areas of depigmentation of the skin, and premature greying of the hair.

Signs of progressive cerebellar and extrapyramidal involvement appear concurrently with the skin lesions. The affected child becomes unsteady on his feet and his speech becomes slurred. His movements become inco-ordinated with an intention tremor and, eventually, choreo-athetosis, mask-like facies, limited eye movements and nystagmus.

Gradual mental deterioration occurs so that mental handicap is obvious by the age of 9 years.

Due to a deficiency of the immunoglobulin IgA, affected children are very susceptible to infections of the lungs and upper respiratory tract. The thymus and lymphoid tissue generally are deficient and there is persistent lymphopenia in many cases and a tendency to develop neoplasms of lymphatic tissue.

There is no specific treatment for this condition and death usually occurs by the age of 20 years.

2. Cerebro-metacarpo-metatarsal Dystrophy (Pseudo-pseudo-hypoparathyroidism, Albright's Syndrome)

The genetics of this condition are not clearly understood but it occurs four times as frequently in females as in males.

Persons affected are below average height and of obese or stocky build, with a broad or round face. The metacarpal and metatarsal bones are shorter than normal. As a result, when the fists are clenched, the metacarpophalangeal line has a characteristic appearance, being concave or straight rather than slightly convex. The nails are hypoplastic.

The serum calcium and phosphorus levels are normal. The EEG is abnormal.

The degree of mental handicap is usually moderately severe.

Dermatoglyphics show a high incidence of arches in the finger tips.

3. Laurence–Moon–Biedl Syndrome

This condition is inherited in an autosomal recessive manner. There is obesity of the Frölich type with hypogenitalism. Extra fingers and toes are present ('polydactyly'). The eyes show various abnormalities— 'retinitis pigmentosa' and often optic atrophy and nystagmus. ('Retinitis pigmentosa' is not, in fact, an inflammatory condition, but rather a degenerative process affecting the rods and cones; which is more accurately described by the term 'tapeto-retinal degeneration'.)Night vision is very poor and vision rapidly deteriorates.

Severe mental handicap is obvious from infancy, but is not progressive.

Dermatoglyphics show an increased incidence of whorls on the finger tips and an extra digital triradius is often present.

4. Tuberous Sclerosis (Epiloia)

This condition is inherited in an autosomal dominant manner, but the gene concerned has poor penetrance so that only partial features of the disease may occur. Its incidence has been estimated at between 1 in 100 000 and 1 in 30 000 live births.

In its fully developed form there are three cardinal signs: mental handicap (usually severe), epilepsy and a facial rash ('adenoma sebaceum'), and an overgrowth of the sebaceous glands, which appears at about the 4th or 5th year of life and which, when fully developed, spreads out from the nose over each cheek in the form of a butterfly's wings and also onto the chin.

There may also be fibromata beneath the finger nails and on the back of the trunk and so-called 'shagreen patches'—raised, flat, thickened areas of skin—in the lumbosacral region, and the skin may show *café-au-lait* or white (depigmented) patches before the development of the facial rash. Flat, oval or circular greyish-white patches ('phakomata') may be seen in the retina.

Smooth muscle tumours may be present in the walls of the heart, and yellowish vascular tumours, consisting of a mixture of smooth muscle, blood vessels and fat, in the kidneys.

Throughout the substance of the brain, and often protruding into the ventricle, there are sclerotic nodules of varying size, consisting of localized overgrowths of neuroglia. These sometimes become calcified and may be visible in radiographs during life. If a child with suggestive skin lesions has a fit, a brain scan may confirm the diagnosis by displaying the nodules before they become calcified and visible at radiography. Radiographs of the lungs may have a honeycomb appearance, due to the presence of many small cysts caused by the growth of multiple small, smooth muscle tumours from the walls of the smaller bronchi and blood vessels.

Various endocrine disturbances have been reported involving thyroid, pituitary–adrenal and carbohydrate metabolism.

The presence of cutaneous signs of the disease in either of the parents of a child with tuberosclerosis indicates that the parent is a heterozygote and that there is a 1 in 2 risk of another child being afflicted.

5. Marinesco–Sjögren Syndrome

This condition is inherited in an autosomal recessive manner.

Affected children are microcephalic and short in stature, with kyphosis, abnormalities of the ribs, broad fingers, talipes equinovarus and pes planus. The hair is scanty or absent and such hair as is present is fine, short and devoid of pigment. Strabismus and cataracts are present and blindness occurs early.

Cerebellar ataxia develops early in life with nystagmus, slurred speech, hypotonia, progressive motor weakness and convulsions.

The degree of mental handicap is severe, but not progressive.

X-LINKED DISORDERS

Apart from those associated with the inborn metabolic disorders there are a number of genetically determined disorders associated with mental handicap which are inherited in a sex-linked or X-linked manner.

1. Oculocerebral Degeneration (Norrie's Disease)

In this rare condition, males develop cataracts and blindness shortly after birth and the eyes degenerate and shrink in size during the first decade. The hearing may also be impaired and epilepsy may occur.

The degree of mental handicap varies.

2. Renpenning's Syndrome

The main characteristic of this syndrome is the normal physical appearance of the affected males. They are severely mentally handicapped with IQs in the 35–50 range.

It has been suggested that Renpenning's syndrome may be responsible for the mental retardation of as many as 10 per cent of males in this IQ range. Some of these cases may be due to the fragile X syndrome.

3. X-Linked Hydrocephalus

In affected males the aqueduct of Sylvius in the brain fails to develop fully and the cerebrospinal fluid accumulates in the ventricles. As a result, the skull becomes enlarged to a variable degree. This enlargement is characteristically globular, and, with the normal-sized face, gives the head the appearance of an inverted pyramid. There may be defects of vision and hearing. In X-linked hydrocephalus the skull and face are frequently asymmetrical. The thumbs are held flexed across the palms and there is spasticity of the legs.

The degree of mental handicap is severe.

The prognosis and treatment of hydrocephalus will be referred to later.

4. X-Linked Spastic Paraplegia

Affected males have a rather fixed facial expression. Nystagmus may be present even at rest, tongue movements are spastic, and the speech is slurred. Paresis and spasticity are more marked in the legs than in the arms, which show athetoid movements. Reflexes are increased and the plantar responses are extensor. It is unusual for wasting of the leg muscles to occur.

The degree of mental handicap is severe.

SYNDROMES WITH A POSSIBLE GENETIC CAUSE

1. 'Happy Puppet' Syndrome

The skull is microcephalic, with flattening and sometimes a horizontal depression in the occipital area. In the eye the choroid is incompletely developed, with optic atrophy. The chin is prominent and the tongue is protruded frequently. The bodily movements are jerky and resemble those of a puppet, with easily provoked and prolonged paroxysms of laughter, hence the name of this syndrome. There is weakness of the limbs and trunk.

Infantile spasms or major fits occur and wave and spike activity is present in electro-encephalograms. Air encephalograms show cerebral atrophy and ventricular dilatations.

The degree of mental handicap is severe.

Steroids and anticonvulsants have produced limited improvement in some cases.

2. de Lange Syndrome

Fetal movements are said to be reduced during pregnancy. At birth, affected children have a low weight for their maturity. Their condition is poor and they often fail to suck or cry. They have a characteristic facial appearance. The eyebrows are bushy and meet across the midline ('synophrys') and the eyelashes are long and curved. The hairline is low on the forehead and the face excessively hairy. The bridge of the nose is depressed and the nostrils face forward. The upper lip is elongated vertically and the mouth droops at the corners. The ears are low-set.

The hands, too, are characteristic. The thumb is proximally placed and, with the short, semi-flexed fingers, gives the hand the appearance of a lobster's claw. More severe deformities of the hands may be present. The elbows cannot be fully extended. Deformities of the feet are less obvious. They tend to be short and to show fusion of the second and third toes ('syndactyly').

The trunk is excessively hairy and the external genitalia are underdeveloped.

The degree of mental handicap is usually severe. Compulsive self-mutilating behaviour similar to that in the Lesch–Nyhan syndrome has been reported.

Dermatoglyphics are helpful in establishing the diagnosis. The fingerprint patterns show an increased frequency of radial loops and a decrease of whorls. The 'atd' angle is intermediate between normal and that in mongolism.

Cases of severe mental handicap have been reported, in which the dwarfism and hirsutism of the de Lange syndrome are associated with dislocation of the radial heads at the elbows and absence of the fifth terminal phalanges, finger nails and toenails.

3. Naevoid Amentia (Sturge–Weber Syndrome)

This is a fairly rare condition in which half of the face, neck and upper part of the chest is covered with a naevus— the so-called 'port-wine stain'. Hemiparesis is present, usually on the opposite side of the body, although both sides may be affected, and epileptic fits occur. The eye on the same side as the naevus is larger than that on the opposite side— 'buphthalmos' or 'ox-eye'.

The facial naevus is associated with an angiomatous growth in the meninges on the corresponding side of the brain and adherent to it.

The degree of mental handicap is usually severe and there may be marked behaviour disorders. The condition has been reported in persons of normal intelligence.

Marked improvement in behaviour and reduction in the frequency of fits sometimes follows operative removal of the meningeal naevus and part or all of the corresponding cerebral hemisphere.

4. Prader–Willi Syndrome

Children with this syndrome are hypotonic from birth. In infancy, the facial appearance is said to be characteristic with the forehead seeming narrow, the eyes having an almond-shaped appearance and strabismus being present. These features become less obvious as the child becomes older, but the unusual smallness of the hands then becomes apparent. In males, hypogenitalism and cryptorchidism occur. By about the age of 2 years, excessive weight gain occurs and by the age of 3 to 5 years, gross obesity is present which cannot be controlled by diets, and diabetes mellitus may develop.

The degree of mental handicap may vary from mild to severe. Affected children are usually affectionate and stable until about 3 years of age, when they often become increasingly stubborn and are subject to temper tantrums. Serious personality disorders persist through adolescence and into adult life and take the form of outbursts of temper and violence with little provocation. Periods of depression may also occur.

It has been suggested that this syndrome may be the result of a developmental defect in the hypothalamus.

INBORN ERRORS OF METABOLISM ASSOCIATED WITH MENTAL HANDICAP

About 80 inborn errors of metabolism known to cause mental handicap have so far been reported. It was thought that they were due to single abnormal genes which each resulted in the absence of a single enzyme leading to the specific metabolic block concerned. It is now clear that each gene is responsible, not for a single enzyme, but for a polypeptide chain, and that the abnormal gene in any inborn metabolic error may exist in two or more different forms or 'alleles' and produce variations in the clinical manifestation of the disorder.

Most of the inborn errors of metabolism are inherited in an autosomal recessive manner but some as X-linked gene defects. The risk to a woman who is a carrier of a recessive gene marrying a man who is the carrier of the same recessive gene has been estimated at 1 in 100, but must vary widely depending upon the different carrier rates in different populations. On the other hand, if they are first cousins the risk is 1 in 8.

Few inborn metabolic errors can be detected by simple tests on the urine and the remainder require specialized pathological techniques including paper and gas chromatography for their detection. Reference will be made later to the antenatal diagnosis of these disorders.

Disorders of Protein Metabolism

Inborn Errors of Amino-acid Metabolism

PRIMARY OVERFLOW AMINO-ACIDURIAS

1. *Phenylketonuria.* At present this is the most common type of known metabolic error associated with mental handicap, occurring once in about 12000 live births. The autosomal recessive gene abnormality causes a deficiency of phenylalanine hydroxylase, the enzyme which takes part in the oxidation of the amino-acid phenylalanine to tyrosine, a precursor of the skin, hair and eye pigment, melanin. As a result of this

deficiency there is an accumulation of phenylalaline in the blood and the excretion of phenylpyruvic acid in the urine, which is said to have a mousey smell.

The presence of phenylpyruvic acid in the urine may be detected by the ferric chloride and 'Phenistix' tests, but the former may give false-positive results and the latter may miss between a quarter and a half of affected children on routine testing between 4 and 6 weeks of age. More reliable is the Guthrie test, which depends on the ability of phenylalanine to promote the growth of *Bacillus subtilis* in the presence of an inhibitory substance in a culture medium. The size of the growth is directly related to the amount of phenylalanine present and this enables accurate quantitative estimations to be made. The test is carried out on filter paper impregnated with blood obtained from pricking a baby's heel between the ages of 6 and 14 days. Earlier testing may give misleadingly low levels in females. Not all babies with raised blood phenylalanine levels are suffering from phenylketonuria. This is the case with some premature babies in whom the serum tyrosine level also is raised initially, but will have returned to normal by the age of 2–3 weeks. Other babies with raised blood phenylalaline levels appear to have a high tolerance for this substance and do not show the classic clinical features of phenyl-ketonuria or suffer brain damage. There is some recent evidence that it is the phenylalanine level in the granular white blood cells which is critical as regards mental development rather than the serum phenylalanine level. It is usual, however, to treat all babies whose blood phenylalanine exceeds 15 mg/100 ml when fasting or after a normal meal or a phenylalanine loading test, or who excrete the characteristic metabolites in their urine when that blood level is exceeded.

Children with phenylketonuria have lower birth weights than their unaffected siblings. Because of the deficiency of melanin they are characteristically fair-haired, fair-skinned and blue-eyed in the races of Northern Europe and lighter in their colouring than their siblings in races with generally more marked pigmentation. They are prone to develop infantile eczema.

Phenylketonuria, if untreated, is always associated with some degree of mental handicap, usually severe, but occasionally very mild. There is, however, no progressive mental deterioration in this condition. About half the affected children never learn to talk and about a third never learn to walk. They sometimes show autistic features, not relating to other people, and resisting cuddling, but becoming unusually attached to small objects. They frequently show mannerisms such as posturing with the hands and rocking backwards and forwards for hours on end.

Between a quarter and a third of patients with phenylketonuria suffer from epilepsy, usually of the grand mal type, but this tends to disappear with age. In the majority of cases there are minor abnormalities in the EEG and also an increased frequency in their near relatives.

39

The development of mental handicap in children in whom phenylketonuria is detected can be prevented by feeding them from birth with diets in which the amount of phenylalanine is restricted so that serum levels are between 2·5 mg and 10 mg per cent, and to which tyrosine and vitamin supplements have been added. The child's progress has to be carefully monitored and its diet adjusted if necessary. If the phenylalanine intake is restricted too severely the child may become fretful, lose its appetite, may vomit and its physical and mental growth are retarded. It may develop a severe rash which fails to respond to all local treatment. Phenylketonuric children on phenylalanine-restricted diets gain weight less rapidly than phenylketonuric children on unrestricted diets.

It has been suggested that, after the age of 3, the brain may be capable of withstanding the harmful effects of raised levels of phenylalanine in the blood so that a return to a normal diet may be made after that age. However, successfully treated phenylketonuric women may have to return to their special diets during pregnancy if damage to the brain of a non-phenylketonuric fetus is to be avoided. Similarly, women who are carriers of the gene for phenylketonuria may have levels of phenylalanine in the blood raised sufficiently to cause fetal damage and may require phenylalanine-restricted diets during pregnancy. A significantly increased percentage of Rhesus-negative women has been reported among the mothers of phenylketonuric children.

Reproduction in successfully treated phenylketonurics carries with it the theoretical possibility of a gradually increasing number of carriers of the gene for phenylketonuria and a consequent increase in the number of sufferers from this condition. This possibility underlines the need for genetic counselling in this and all other abnormal conditions with a known genetic basis.

2. *Homocystinuria*. At present homocystinuria would appear to be the second most common inborn error of amino-acid metabolism known to cause mental handicap, occurring about a quarter as frequently as phenylketonuria. It is inherited in an autosomal recessive manner and results in deficiency of the enzyme cystathionine synthetase, which normally takes part in the conversion of the amino-acid methionine to cystine. In homocystinuria the process is arrested at the stage between homocystine and cystathionine. The levels of both methionine and homocystine are raised in the blood, and homocystine is excreted in the urine, which is said to have a sulphurous odour. Homocystine may be detected in the urine by the cyanide nitroprusside test.

The physical signs of homocystinuria are fair hair and skin, dislocation of the lenses of the eyes, a characteristic flush of the cheeks, enlarged joints, knock-knees and a shuffling gait. The peripheral circulation is poor, with well-marked livido reticularis and a tendency for various thrombo-embolic phenomena to occur. These signs of homocystinuria are not obvious at birth and, as the child becomes older, osteoporosis may occur and the skeletal abnormalities may become more marked and resemble those of Marfan's syndrome, in which mental handicap is rare, with a high arched palate, chest deformities and long narrow fingers. The liver undergoes fatty degeneration and fits are frequent. Early mental development is usually normal but signs of gross deterioration appear in the most severe cases in the first year of life. It is more common for mental deterioration to become obvious at about the time of starting school but homocystinuria is not incompatible with normal intelligence in adult life. Homocystinuria may sometimes present with schizophrenia-like symptoms.

The development of mental handicap may be prevented by treatment with a diet low in methionine and supplemented with cystine. A proportion of cases respond to the administration of pyridoxine without the necessity for these dietary restrictions. In such cases there appears to be no deficiency of cystathionine synthetase.

3. *Argininosuccinic Aciduria*. This condition is inherited in an autosomal recessive manner. There is a deficiency of the enzyme arginosuccinase, which normally takes part in the conversion of the amino-acid argininosuccinic acid into arginine and fumaric acid. As a result argininosuccinic acid accumulates in the blood and appears in the urine. Blood ammonia levels are also raised. Argininosuccinic aciduria may be detected by enzyme estimations in amniotic cell cultures and carriers may be detected by argininosuccinase estimations in their red blood cells.

The most striking physical signs in this condition are related to the absence of arginine, which is normally present in hair. The hair is abnormally brittle, so that its length never exceeds 5–10 mm. On examination each hair shows irregularly alternating spindle-like swellings and strictures ('monilethrix'). The nails, also, may be brittle and various skin disorders may be present. Affected children show an early refusal to eat protein and develop clonic spasms and convulsions and later choreiform movements and mild ataxia.

The degree of mental handicap may be severe, but in mild examples of this condition the hair abnormalities may be the only sign of the disorder.

Treatment consists of restricting the protein intake, but results have, so far, been disappointing.

Monilethrix occurs also in Menkes' syndrome ('kinky hair disease'), which is inherited in an X-linked manner. Affected male infants fail to thrive. They are microcephalic, with micrognathia and a high arched palate. The hair on the scalp is sparse, coarse, stubbly, kinky and white, due to absence of pigment.

The degree of mental handicap is severe, and progressive mental deterioration occurs, with convulsions, increasing spasticity, and death in a state of decerebrate rigidity by the age of about 3 years.

The nature of the underlying metabolic disorder is not known but paper chromatography has shown an increase in glutamic acid in some cases.

4. *Arginaemia.* This condition is very much rarer than argininosuccinic aciduria and its mode of inheritance is not known with certainty. It is due to a deficiency of the enzyme arginase, which is responsible for the metabolism of arginine, which accumulates in the blood in this condition. The blood ammonia levels are also raised.

Affected children have spastic paraplegia and convulsions and are severely mentally handicapped.

In spite of its apparent rarity this condition is of particular interest in view of the possibility of its effective treatment, not by dietary restrictions as in other inborn metabolic errors, but by the replacement of the missing enzyme, arginase. Arginase is synthesized by the Shope papilloma virus, which is harmless to man. It has been injected into two sisters suffering from arginaemia in the hope of overcoming the metabolic block and reducing their blood arginine levels to normal.

5. *Citrullinuria.* It is probable that this, so far very rare condition, is inherited in an autosomal recessive manner. Due to the deficiency of the enzyme argininosuccinic acid synthetase, citrulline accumulates in the blood and appears in the urine with a number of other amino-acids in considerably increased concentrations.

The condition manifests itself during the first year of life in attacks of vomiting, generalized convulsions, arrested development and subsequent regression to a severely mentally handicapped level, with marked irritability.

So far no treatment has been devised to prevent the mental deterioration, but vomiting and convulsions may cease and the child become more responsive and less irritable if the protein in his diet is restricted.

6. *Cystathioninuria.* It is probable that this condition is inherited in an autosomal recessive manner, but it has been suggested that it may be caused by a dominant gene of variable penetrance. Cystathionine, like homocystine, is an intermediate product in the conversion of methionine to cystine, but in cystathioninuria the block is at a later stage of the metabolic process. The block is due to a deficiency of the enzyme cystathionase. Cystathionine accumulates in the blood and appears in the urine.

The growth of affected children is arrested and they tend to be anaemic and to have persistent thrombocytopenia. The degree of mental handicap varies widely in individual cases.

Treatment consists of administering pyridoxine, which increases the growth rate and reduces, if not prevents, the degree of mental handicap. To protect the developing fetus, mothers who are heterozygous for this condition should be given pyridoxine throughout their pregnancies.

7. *Histidinaemia.* This condition is inherited in an autosomal recessive manner. There is a deficiency of the enzyme histidine ammonia lyase, which is necessary for the conversion of histidine to urocanic acid, a precursor of glutamic acid. Histidine accumulates in the blood and it appears in the urine with considerable amounts of imidazole pyruvic acid and imidazole acetic acid. The importance of imidazole pyruvic acid is that it may give a false-positive reaction to the 'Phenistix' and ferric chloride tests and lead to errors in diagnosis.

Many of the affected children are fair-haired and blue-eyed. The degree of mental impairment varies considerably. Some cases are severely mentally handicapped, others are within the normal range of intelligence, but all have in common speech defects.

Treatment consists of restricting the amount of histidine in the diet, from early infancy onwards, so as to minimize the risk of inevitable brain damage and mental impairment.

8. *Hydroxykynureninuria.* The mode of inheritance of this disorder is not known with certainty. There is a deficiency of the enzyme kynureninase, which is necessary for the conversion of kynurenine to 3-hydroxy-anthranilic acid, a precursor of nicotinic acid. As a result, there are signs of nicotinic acid deficiency and growth is stunted.

The degree of mental handicap may be only slight and some cases may be normal in intelligence.

Treatment with large doses of pyridoxine, with nicotinic acid supplements, may improve the physical condition, but the effect on the mental condition is uncertain.

9. *Hydroxylysinuria.* The mode of inheritance and the nature of the metabolic disorder in this condition are not fully understood. The level of hydroxylisine is raised in the blood and urine.

Affected children tend to be hyperactive and to have myoclonic and major motor seizures. Their degree of mental handicap is severe.

No effective treatment of this condition is known.

10. *Hydroxyprolinaemia.* The mode of inheritance and the nature of the metabolic disorder in this condition are not yet fully understood, but it is known to be associated with a deficiency of the enzyme hydroxyproline oxidase.

Affected children are retarded in their development and suffer from attacks of haematuria. They are severely mentally handicapped and hyperactive.

No effective treatment of this condition is known.

11. *Hyperammonaemia.* This condition is inherited in an autosomal recessive manner. It is a disorder of the urea cycle, due to a deficiency of the enzyme ornithine transcarbamylase, leading to an accumulation of ammonia in the blood.

Symptoms appear when the child is weaned from breast to cow's milk, at which time it develops anorexia and starts to vomit. At first irritable, it later becomes lethargic and develops convulsions and has episodes of extreme muscular rigidity with intermittent opisthotonus. The liver becomes progressively enlarged.

The degree of mental handicap is severe.

Treatment consists of limiting the daily protein intake to less than 1·5 g per kg body weight, in frequent small feeds.

12. *Hyperglycinaemia.* This condition is probably inherited in an autosomal recessive manner. The exact nature of the metabolic disorder in this condition is not known, but the level of glycine in the blood is raised and it appears in the urine with increased amounts of glyoxylic acid and oxalic acid.

Affected children are retarded in their growth and develop epilepsy shortly after birth.

The degree of mental handicap is severe.

Treatment with a protein-restricted diet reduces the frequency of the fits and prolongs the child's life, but mental handicap may not be prevented.

13. *Hyperlysinaemia.* This condition is inherited in an autosomal recessive manner. There is a deficiency of the enzyme lysine-ketoglutamate reductase, resulting in an increase in the amount of lysine in both blood and urine, and the amount of other amino-acids is also increased in the urine. The blood ammonia level rises.

Affected children have feeding difficulties due to impaired swallowing. The liver and spleen enlarge progressively. The hair is brittle. Severe convulsions occur with hypertonia and flexion spasms in between. The degree of mental handicap varies. There is no known effective treatment.

14. *Hyperprolinaemia.* The mode of inheritance and the nature of the metabolic disorder in this condition are not yet fully understood, but it is known to be associated with a deficiency of the enzyme proline oxidase.

Early development is usually normal and then feeding difficulties occur and frequent generalized convulsions develop. Marked deafness is present, and persistent haematuria and attacks of pyuria occur in association with defective renal development. The EEG is abnormally sensitive to photic stimulation.

Mental development varies from severe mental handicap to superior intelligence.

No effective treatment of this condition is known.

15. *Hypervalinaemia.* It is probable that this condition is inherited in an autosomal recessive manner. There is a deficiency of the enzyme valine transaminase, which is necessary for the conversion of lysine to alpha-keto-isovaleric acid.

Affected children have difficulty in sucking, have attacks of vomiting and fail to thrive. Blindness may occur. The degree of mental handicap is variable.

44

A diet in which the amounts of valine, leucine and isoleucine are restricted may improve the physical condition, but its effect on the mental state is uncertain.

16. *Maple Syrup Urine Disease.* This disease is so called because of the characteristic smell of the urine, which is said to resemble that of maple syrup. Its frequency has been estimated at about 1 per 250 000 live births. It is inherited in an autosomal recessive manner.

There is a deficiency of the enzyme ketoacid decarboxylase, causing a disturbance of the metabolism of the branched-chain amino-acids (BCAA) valine, leucine, isoleucine and allo-isoleucine, which are present in the blood and urine in abnormal amounts. The reaction of the urine to the ferric chloride test may be mistaken for that of phenyl-ketonuria, but the two conditions may be clearly differentiated by paper chromatography.

Maple syrup disease manifests itself in the first week of life. The infant becomes irritable, has difficulty in sucking and swallowing and breathes in a jerky manner. If untreated, signs of progressive cerebral involvement occur: convulsions, paralyses, rigidity and opisthotonus, leading to death in a few months.

There is an intermittent form of this disease, in which the typical urine is excreted only during infections and in which the degree of mental handicap may be minimal or absent.

Treatment consists of a synthetic diet containing the minimum amounts of leucine, isoleucine and valine necessary to maintain their normal levels in the blood. Very early diagnosis is essential for treatment to be effective. As with any other synthetic diet, growth may be retarded. Some cases respond to thiamine hydrochloride without any dietary restrictions.

17. *Oculocerebro-renal Syndrome* (*Lowe's Syndrome*). It is probable that this condition is inherited in an X-linked manner. The exact nature of the metabolic disorder is not known, but there is a decreased ability of the renal tubules to regulate the acid–base balance, with resulting acidosis.

A number of amino-acids are excreted in the urine, but the paper chromatography pattern is not specific.

Affected children develop anorexia, and growth is severely retarded, with osteomalacia and, later, rickets developing. Cataracts are present from birth and there is generalized hypotonia. Cryptorchidism is a common feature. Affected children are said to have a characteristic appearance, with a dome-shaped head with frontal bossing and large eyes sunk well into their sockets. The thoracic diameter is increased and the upper abdomen is protuberant due to the chronic hyperventilation provoked by the acidosis.

Many affected children die in early infancy. Those that survive are severely mentally handicapped. There is no effective treatment of the underlying biochemical disorder, but in some cases the resulting rickets may be successfully treated with vitamin D and alkali, and these cases may survive into early childhood.

18. *Ornithinaemia.* The mode of inheritance of this condition is not known with certainty. It is due to a deficiency of the enzyme ornithine keto-acid transaminase, which is responsible for the metabolism of ornithine to γ-glutamylsemialdehyde, a precursor of glutamic acid. As a result there is an increase in the level of ornithine in the blood and a marked generalized amino-aciduria, especially of proline and valine, but not of ornithine. Glycosuria occurs due to renal tubular damage.

Affected children fail to thrive during infancy and are retarded in their development of speech. They develop cirrhosis of the liver.

The degree of mental handicap may vary from the severe to the mild.

The effectiveness of treatment by restricting the ornithine intake is not yet proved.

19. *Ornithine Transcarbamylase Deficiency.* The mode of inheritance of this condition is not known with certainty, but there is some evidence that it may be X-linked. As a result of the deficiency of the enzyme ornithine transcarbamylase the synthesis of citrulline is defective. Ammonia accumulates in the blood.

Affected children are retarded in their growth and subject to attacks of vomiting and screaming and, later, lethargy and stupor. The development of speech is delayed.

The degree of mental handicap is severe.

Treatment consists of limiting the dietary protein and giving citric acid and aspartic acid supplements in order to reduce the blood ammonia levels and minimize the degree of brain damage.

20. *Tryptophanuria.* The mode of inheritance of this condition is not known with certainty, nor is the exact nature of the metabolic disorder. The level of tryptophan is raised in both blood and urine.

Affected children are retarded in their growth, and hyperpigmentation and thickening of the skin develops by about the 6th month.

The degree of mental handicap is severe.

There is no known effective treatment.

RENAL (TRANSPORT) AMINO-ACIDURIAS

1. *Hartnup Disease.* This condition is inherited in an autosomal recessive manner. There is a deficit in the transport of amino-acids across the mucous membranes of the intestines and across the epithelium of the renal tubules. In particular, tryptophan absorption is grossly defective and results in a deficiency of nicotinic acid, of which it is a precursor. There is an abnormal excretion in the urine of a number of amino-acids, which produce a characteristic pattern on paper chromatography. The urine always contains also a large amount of

indole-3-acetic acid and usually a large amount of indican. There is a moderate increase of protoporphyrin in the faeces.

The most constant clinical feature of this condition is photosensitivity, with the development of a rash identical with that in pellagra on exposure to the sun, i.e. there is roughening, reddening and, in some cases, cracking and ulceration of the skin of the exposed areas of the body, raised above and sharply defined from the unaffected skin.

In untreated cases there is a great loss of weight, and the neurological signs of pellagra may occur, with mental confusion and ataxia prominent. Diarrhoea is not a constant feature.

Children in whom the metabolic abnormality is present are mentally handicapped to varying degrees, even if the obvious 'pellagroid' signs are not present. The neurological and skin signs dramatically disappear and the weight returns to normal with the administration of large doses of nicotinamide, but there is no improvement in intelligence and the abnormal excretion of amino-acids persists.

2. *Methionine Malabsorption (Oast House Urine) Syndrome.* It is thought that this condition is inherited in an autosomal recessive manner. The primary disorder is an inability to absorb methionine from the gut. Bacterial fermentation of methionine then occurs and leads to an accumulation of the keto-acids and hydroxy-acids of phenylalanine, tyrosine, leucine and methionine in the blood and their excretion in the urine, which has a smell said to resemble that of beer, dry celery or burnt sugar.

Affected children have feeding difficulties and fail to thrive. They resemble children with phenylketonuria in having fair hair and blue eyes. They suffer from attacks of diarrhoea and convulsions.

The degree of mental handicap is severe.

Early treatment with a methionine-restricted diet may improve the physical condition and prevent the development of mental handicap.

Disorders of Carbohydrate Metabolism

1. *Galactosaemia*

This condition is inherited in an autosomal recessive manner. There is a deficiency or absence of the enzyme phosphogalactose uridyl transferase, which is necessary for the conversion of galactose-1-phosphate to glucose. As a result, there is an accumulation of galactose and galactose-1-phosphate in the blood, which damages the liver and kidneys, and galactose appears in the urine, as well as a number of amino-acids. The enzyme deficiency may be detected by estimations on amniotic cell cultures, but there is no simple routine ward test which is specific for the presence of galactose in the urine.

In severe cases symptoms appear in the first 2 weeks of life. The infant starts to vomit and becomes increasingly lethargic and reluctant to feed, loses weight and becomes jaundiced. If the condition is untreated, cirrhosis of the liver and cataracts develop and the child is severely subnormal and death occurs early. However, if the condition is diagnosed and treated shortly after birth by a galactose-free-diet, the cataracts disappear, liver function returns to normal and the severity of mental handicap may be reduced, if not entirely prevented.

2. *Glycogen Storage Disorders*

This group of disorders is inherited in an autosomal recessive manner. In most members of the group, hypoglycaemia occurs, due either to an inability to form normal glycogen or to convert stored glycogen into glucose. For some disorders in this group there is no known treatment and death occurs in infancy or early childhood, but in the following the child may survive long enough for his mental condition to cause concern:

a. 'DEBRANCHER' DEFICIENCY

This condition is so called because there is a deficiency of the enzyme amylo-1,6-glucosidase, which is necessary for the breakdown of glycogen to glucose at the stage of cleavage at the points at which the glycogen molecule branches. As a result, abnormal glycogen accumulates in the tissues and blood levels of glucose are inadequate. The hypoglycaemia is increased in this condition because there is also a deficiency of the liver enzyme glucose-6-phosphatase, which is necessary for the release of glucose from glucose-6-phosphate.

Affected children have poor appetites and fail to thrive, so that growth is retarded and bone maturation is delayed. The liver becomes greatly enlarged and there are signs of malnutrition and emaciation. Recurrent respiratory infections occur. Convulsions, brain damage and severe mental handicap result from the prolonged hypoglycaemia.

Glucose-6-phosphatase activity may be increased by the administration of triamcinolone, but there is no known way of increasing amylo-1,6-glucosidase activity.

b. GLYCOGENOSIS

It is believed that this condition is due to a deficiency of the enzyme phosphorylase kinase, which is responsible for activating the liver enzyme phosphorylase. As a result, excessive amounts of abnormal glycogen accumulate in the liver and brain, and it is this that causes the damage rather than hypoglycaemia, which does not occur in this condition.

Affected children fail to thrive and are obviously retarded in reaching their developmental milestones. The liver becomes enlarged, cataracts may occur, and there are convulsions, signs of progressive brain damage, such as ataxia, nystagmus and cerebral palsy, with severe mental handicap.

It is possible that early treatment with glucagon might diminish the degree of brain damage by preventing excessive glycogen deposition.

3. *Hypoglycemosis (or Idiopathic Hypoglycaemia)*

It is now thought that this condition is inherited in an autosomal dominant manner. Affected individuals have an abnormal sensitivity to leucine, which produces a rapid and prolonged fall in blood glucose and an excessive rise in plasma insulin.

Affected children develop convulsions in infancy and irreversible brain damage and severe mental handicap, if prolonged hypoglycaemia is not treated early. Treatment consists of restricting leucine in the diet and giving extra glucose between feeds. ACTH may be necessary in severe cases. Fortunately, the leucine sensitivity is self-limiting and, by the age of 5 years, it may be possible for the child to resume a normal unrestricted diet.

4. *Familial Lactic Acidosis*

The mode of inheritance and the exact nature of the underlying metabolic disorder in this condition are not known with certainty. There is both an excessive production of lactic acid by erythrocytes and muscles and a deficient ability to metabolize it normally, with a resultant accumulation in the blood.

The condition manifests itself in the second year of life as attacks of hypernoea at rest, muscular twitching, progressive ataxia, convulsions, and mental deterioration, leading to death in about 6 months.

There is as yet no known specific treatment.

Disorders of Lipid Metabolism

In this group of metabolic disorders there is abnormal storage of lipids in the tissues leading to their degeneration.

1. *Cerebromacular Degeneration (Amaurotic Familial Idiocy)*

Disorders in this rare group are inherited in an autosomal recessive manner and are characterized clinically by progressive mental and visual deterioration.

a. SPHINGOLIPIDOSES

i. *Tay–Sachs' Disease.* This condition is due to a deficiency of the enzyme hexosaminadase A, which results in an accumulation of ganglioside GM2 in the tissues. It occurs most frequently in Ashkenazi Jews, in whom the carrier rate is as high as 1 in 25. The onset is during the 1st year of life, often as early as the 3rd month, and the course of the disease is progressive mental deterioration, blindness, convulsions and death within 2 years. Optic atrophy occurs, with the pathognomonic 'cherry-red spot' at the macula lutea. Hearing, however, remains acute until the terminal stages of the disease. There is progressive spastic paralysis affecting all muscles with, in some cases, a condition of cerebral rigidity just before death.

This disease occurs also both in a late infantile, and in a juvenile form, in which the onset may be delayed until the 5th and 7th year of life in children whose previous development has been normal. The subsequent course is similar to that of the infantile form, although slower, with death occurring usually between the ages of 14 and 18 years.

There is no known treatment for this disease, but its incidence may be reduced by the termination of pregnancies in which a deficiency of hexosaminadase A is found in fibroblast cultures from amniotic fluid, and by the detection of carriers whose blood shows a similar, but less severe, deficiency of the enzyme.

ii. *Niemann–Pick Disease.* This condition is due to a deficiency of the enzyme sphingomyelinase, which is necessary for the normal breakdown of sphingomyelin, which accumulates in excess in the tissues in this disease.

The onset and course of the disease are similar to those in Tay–Sachs' disease. As in that disease, the 'cherry-red spot' is present, but in addition there is marked enlargement of the liver and spleen, with pigmentation of the skin. This enlargement is due to infiltration with Niemann–Pick cells, which spread to all the organs in the body.

There is no known treatment of this disease, but antenatal diagnosis and the detection of carriers are possible by enzyme estimation.

iii. *Generalized Gangliosidosis.* In this condition there is a deficiency of the enzyme GMI ganglioside β-galactosidase, which results in an accumulation of GMI ganglioside in the brain, liver, spleen and kidneys.

The onset and course of this disease is similar to that of the late infantile form of Tay–Sachs' disease, with death occurring within the first 2 years of life.

There is no known treatment, but antenatal diagnosis and the detection of carriers are possible by enzyme estimations.

b. NEURONAL CEROID-LIPOFUCINOSES

This group of disorders is inherited in an autosomal recessive manner and has in common the presence of large amounts of yellow brown granules, which appear to be a type of ceroid-lipofuscin pigment, in the cells of the brain and retina, which degenerate as a result. The nature of the underlying biochemical disorder is not known.

The late juvenile (Bielchowsky–Jansky disease) and juvenile (Batten–Vogt disease or Spielmeyer–Sjögren disease) forms are associated with mental handicap.

i. *Bielchowsky–Jansky Disease.* The onset is between the ages of 1 and 4 years, with severe convulsions, signs of cerebellar dysfunction, optic atrophy and mental deterioration, with death within a few years.

ii. *Batten–Vogt Disease; Spielmeyer–Sjögren Disease.* In this disease the onset is between the ages of 5 and 10 years, and its progress is slower, with retinitis pigmentosa and visual loss, spasticity, extra-pyramidal signs, mental deterioration and the late onset of convulsions.

There is no known treatment for either of these diseases.

2. *Cerebrosidoses*

a. GAUCHER'S DISEASE

This condition is inherited in an autosomal recessive manner. There is a deficiency of the enzyme cerebroside β-glucosidase, which results in an accumulation of various cerebrosides (Gaucher cells) in the brain, liver, spleen and other tissues of the body, including the bone marrow.

The onset of this condition is within the first 6 months of life, with signs of rapid deterioration of the brain and mental deterioration, with death at about the age of 1 year in a state of decerebrate rigidity.

There is no known treatment of this disease, but the enzyme deficiency may be detected in fibroblast cultures obtained by amniocentesis and by blood level estimations on carriers.

b. METACHROMATIC LEUCODYSTROPHY

This condition is inherited in an autosomal recessive manner. There is a deficiency of the enzyme cerebroside sulphate sulphatase, which is necessary for the breakdown of sulphatide (ceramide-galactose-3-sulphate), a normal component of myelin. As a result of the deficiency there is a progressive accumulation of sulphatide in both the grey and white matter of the brain, in the peripheral nerve tissue, liver, gall bladder and kidney, and metachromatic granules appear in various tissues and in the urine. Myelin degeneration is followed by axon degeneration and neuroglial overgrowth.

The onset is usually after the 1st year of life and the course is marked by slowly progressive failure of hearing, speech and vision, muscular inco-ordination, epilepsy, mental deterioration and spastic paralysis, leading to decerebrate rigidity and death within 5–10 years.

There is no known treatment of this disease, but antenatal diagnosis and the detection of carriers is possible by enzyme estimations.

3. *Refsum's Disease*

This condition is inherited in an autosomal recessive manner. There is a deficiency of the enzyme phytanic acid oxidase, as a result of which there is a failure to convert phytol (a major constituent of the chlorophyll molecule) to carbon dioxide and an accumulation of the intermediate metabolite phytanic acid in many tissues, including the brain and the peripheral nerves. This leads to defective synthesis of myelin, a gradual loss of the myelin sheath and perineural fibrosis.

The onset may occur in childhood, when there may be progressive failure of vision, associated with retinitis pigmentosa and progressive nerve deafness. Ataxia, nystagmus and other cerebellar signs develop. Symmetrical weakness of the distal parts of the limbs occurs, with weakness of the deep reflexes.

Mental development is arrested and followed by varying degrees of mental deterioration.

In addition to the signs of damage to the central nervous system, ichthyosis (scaliness of the skin) occurs.

The degree of mental and physical deterioration may be reduced by giving a phytanic acid-free diet and vitamin A and E supplements.

Antenatal diagnosis and the detection of carriers are possible by enzyme estimations.

Disorders of Connective Tissue

1. *Mucopolysaccharidoses*

Six different types are described in this group of disorders and are designated as MPS Types I–VI. Only in Types I–III is mental handicap a constant feature. In each, abnormal storage of mucopolysaccharides occurs in the connective tissues, which undergo degeneration. It has been suggested that there is a link between the mucopolysaccharidoses and the lipidoses.

a. MUCOPOLYSACCHARIDOSIS TYPE I (HURLER'S SYNDROME— GARGOYLISM)

This condition is inherited in an autosomal recessive manner. The exact nature of the enzyme defect is not known, but large quantities of chondroitin sulphate B and heparitin sulphate are excreted in the urine.

The physical signs of this condition are not obvious at birth, but develop during the 1st year of life. By this time the facial appearance is characteristic and is said to resemble that of a gargoyle. The head is large and may be generally misshapen, but typically there is frontal bossing, with prominent supra-orbital ridges and a depressed bridge of the nose. The sella turcica is elongated. The eyebrows are coarse and bushy, the ears are set low, the tongue is large, fissured and constantly protruded. The dentition is delayed and irregular. About 75 per cent of these patients show various degrees of corneal opacity, and defects of ocular movements and of balance are common. The neck is short and thick and the dorsal spine kyphotic owing to abnormal vertebral growth, which produces a characteristic 'beaked' appearance on radiographic examination. The centres of ossification are delayed and the patient is short in stature and the limbs are relatively short, with limitation of extension of the joints.

The liver and spleen are greatly enlarged, with distension of the abdomen and often umbilical hernia. Congenital cardiac lesions are often present.

Mental development is arrested and the child undergoes progressive mental and physical deterioration and dies early in the second decade.

A hopeful development in the treatment of these children is the reported success of bone-marrow transplant. Although carrying a degree of risk because of host-versus-graft reactions, a number of these transplants have now taken place, with subsequent production of the missing enzyme and apparently normal development of the children. Existing physical abnormalities have regressed.

If this treatment is as successful as the first promising reports suggest, it may well open up new horizons for the treatment of other inborn errors of metabolism.

The excess of heparitin sulphate and the presence of metachromatic granules in cells may be detected during pregnancy by amniocentesis and the possibility of termination of pregnancy considered.

b. MUCOPOLYSACCHARIDOSIS TYPE II (HUNTER'S SYNDROME—GARGOYLISM)

This condition is inherited in an X-linked manner, and is about one-fifth as common as Hurler's syndrome. As in that condition, the exact nature of the enzyme defect is not known, and large quantities of chondroitin sulphate B and heparitin sulphate are excreted in the urine. The facial appearance is similar in the two conditions, but in Hunter's syndrome corneal clouding does not occur, but nerve deafness is present in about 40 per cent of cases, and dwarfing is less common than in Hurler's syndrome.

Mental deterioration occurs more slowly than in Hurler's syndrome.

The same comments on possible treatment apply as in the case of Hurler's syndrome. The excess of heparitin sulphate may be detected during pregnancy by amniocentesis and the possibility of termination of pregnancy considered. Carriers may be detected by the presence of metachromatic granules in cultured skin fibroblasts.

c. MUCOPOLYSACCHARIDOSIS TYPE III (SANFILIPPO SYNDROME)

This condition is inherited in an autosomal recessive manner. The exact nature of the enzyme defect is not known, but large amounts of heparitin sulphate are excreted in the urine. The physical signs of this disease are less marked than those in Hurler's and Hunter's syndromes. The skull is obviously enlarged and very thick, and deafness frequently occurs. There is moderate dwarfing, the joints are stiffened and the liver may be moderately enlarged. In contrast to the mildness of the physical signs, the degree of mental handicap is severe, with considerable intellectual deterioration by the age of 5.

The same comments on possible treatment apply as in the case of Hurler's syndrome. The excess of heparitin sulphate may be detected during pregnancy by amniocentesis and the possibility of termination of pregnancy considered.

Other Inborn Errors of Metabolism

1. *Glucose-6-phosphate-dehydrogenase (G6PD) Deficiency*

This condition occurs most frequently in Negro races in whom it is inherited in an X-linked manner. As a result of the deficiency of G6PD, affected males are predisposed to develop an haemolytic anaemia when drugs such as aspirin, sulphonamides or some antimalarial drugs are administered. The resulting damage to the brain may be sufficient to cause mental handicap. The jaundice may be present at birth if the mother has taken such drugs during pregnancy. Further brain damage may be prevented by avoiding the administration of the types of drugs mentioned.

2. *Hepatolenticular Degeneration (Wilson's Disease)*

This condition is inherited in an autosomal recessive manner. It is a disorder of copper metabolism in which there is both excessive absorption of copper from the diet and a deficiency of the normal copper-carrying protein, caeruloplasmin. As a result, there is greatly increased excretion of copper in the urine, with renal damage and a generalized amino-aciduria, proteinuria and glycosuria.

The signs of hepatolenticular degeneration occur most frequently in the second decade, in a child who has previously been mentally normal, but who may have failed to thrive and suffered from jaundice. Involuntary choreiform movements with tremor develop and there is progressive difficulty in articulation and in swallowing. Rigidity of the muscles of the limbs, trunk and face occurs, followed by contractures and gradual muscle wasting.

The physical signs are associated with degeneration in the lenticular nuclei of the brain, due to copper deposition and grossly disturbed function of the liver, which develops polylobular cirrhosis from the same cause.

A smoky brownish ring ('Kayser-Fleischer ring'), due to deposits of copper at the outer margin of the cornea, is pathognomonic of this condition, and so-called 'sunflower cataracts', due to copper deposits in the lens capsule, are rare accompaniments.

Hyperpigmentation may occur on the front of the legs, due to the increased deposition of melanin in the basal layer of the epidermis possibly as the result of the disturbed liver function.

If untreated, there is progressive mental deterioration, and paranoid psychosis with hallucinations may occur. Emaciation in the acute form leads to death in 3–7 years. Early treatment may prevent physical and mental deterioration. Treatment is directed at reducing the absorption of copper by limiting it in the diet and by administering potassium sulphide, and by mobilizing the excess copper from the tissues to be excreted in the urine by administering the chelating agents D-penicillamine and dimercaprol. The use of L-dopa and triethylene tetramine dihydrochloride has been claimed to be effective in cases where the other chelating agents fail.

3. *Hypothyroidism* (*Cretinism*)

It is now believed that as many as five distinct inborn metabolic errors may cause the clinical picture of this condition. All result in a deficiency of the thyroid gland secretion, thyroxine. The mode of inheritance is not known with certainty, but in three it is believed to be in an autosomal recessive manner. Thyroxine obtained from the mother during pregnancy is sufficient to prevent the signs of the condition manifesting themselves at birth, but insufficient to protect the fetal brain and skeleton completely from the effects of lack of thyroxine. Unfortunately, if diagnosis and treatment are delayed until after the age of 3 months, the chances of preventing irreparable brain damage become progressively less.

Early clinical signs are apathy and lethargy in feeding, partly due to enlargement of the tongue, which also causes noisy breathing. Frequently, the feeding problems are the only complaints about the baby the mother may have at this stage. If untreated, the baby becomes increasingly slow and does not readily laugh or smile. The skin becomes yellowish, loose and wrinkled, with marked puffiness of the skin and thickening of the eyelids, nostrils, lips, feet and back of the neck, which is short and thick. Fatty pads develop above the clavicles, in the axillae and between the scapulae. The abdomen becomes protuberant and umbilical hernia may occur. The hair of the head and eyebrows is scanty. The temperature is subnormal and the baby emits a characteristic leathery cry.

Later, the baby makes no attempt to sit up, stand or walk at the normal ages. The epiphyses are delayed in their appearance, growth is stunted and the anterior fontanelle may still be open in adult life. Speech may not appear until as late as 7 or 8 years of age. Sexual development may be delayed or incomplete.

In untreated cases there is inevitably mental handicap. The institution of treatment after the age of 3 months may allow mental and physical development to progress subsequently, but it is doubtful whether the previous defect of intelligence is ever made good completely, although the physical appearance may become completely normal.

4. *Infantile Hyperuricaemia (Lesch–Nyhan–Syndrome)*

This condition is inherited in an X-linked manner. There is a deficiency of the enzyme hypoxanthine-guanine phosphoribosyl transferase (HGPRT), as a result of which there is a disturbance of purine metabolism, leading to an accumulation of uric acid in the blood and severe brain damage.

Affected males develop normally until they are a few weeks old, when they give an excessive 'startle' reaction with attacks of hypertonia. Spasticity increases and cerebral palsy and choreo-athetosis develop and mental deterioration is progressive. The appetite is poor, but the thirst is excessive and attacks of haematuria may occur. Death usually occurs before puberty.

A particularly distressing feature of this disorder is the tendency to extreme self-mutilation, which takes the form of chewing their lips away and biting the fingers down to the bone in spite of the obvious pain they cause themselves. While they are doing this, the children seem to be terrified and are obviously relieved when restrained.

The administration of allopurinol reduces the level of uric acid in the blood, but does not prevent or reduce the degree of brain damage, for which there is no known treatment. However, the condition may be detected during pregnancy by enzyme estimations on fibroblast cultures obtained by amniocentesis and termination of pregnancy considered.

5. *Nephrogenic Diabetes Insipidus*

This condition is inherited in an X-linked manner and, except in rare cases, affects only males. The exact nature of the metabolic disorder is not known, but there is a complete failure of the kidney tubules to respond to the posterior pituitary hormone, pitressin. As a result, there is a failure of control of the passage of water from the blood to the kidneys. Soon after birth the child passes large volumes of urine, develops an excessive thirst, vomits, becomes dehydrated and has frequent convulsions and may run erratic fevers.

This condition, which persists throughout life, causes mental handicap unless the dehydration is prevented by a continuous large water intake. Fluid loss may be considerably reduced by administering ethacrynic acid with potassium chloride supplements.

Carriers may be detected by urine concentration tests on women in whom the condition is suspected.

Ichthyosis

Ichthyosis (scaliness of the skin) is a feature of the following three conditions associated with mental handicap, which may be due to inborn errors of metabolism:

1. *Rud's Syndrome*

This is inherited in an autosomal recessive manner. Mental handicap, ichthyosis, dwarfism, infantilism, epilepsy, polyneuritis and anaemia are present.

2. *X-linked Ichthyosis*

Mental handicap, ichthyosis and hypogonadism are present in males only, except in very rare cases.

3. *Sjögren–Larsson Syndrome*

This is inherited in an autosomal recessive manner. Mental handicap, ichthyosis, macular degeneration of the retina and spastic paraplegia are present and convulsions may occur. Sweating is absent except on the face and the backs of the hands.

CASES OF AMENTIA WITHOUT KNOWN GENETIC CAUSES

A number of cases of amentia are attributable more directly to environmental than to genetic causes. These causes may operate during either pregnancy or labour or subsequently at any time before the genetically determined limits of intelligence have been reached. They include anything which can interfere with the nutrition or oxygenation of the brain or may destroy previously normal brain cells.

The growth of the brain does not proceed at an even rate throughout intra-uterine life, but takes place in two spurts of activity. During the first, which occurs between the 15th and 20th week of gestation, the neurons are multiplying to reach their adult number, and during the second, which starts at the 25th week and continues until the second year of postnatal life, glial cell multiplication is taking place. The weight of the developing brain is directly correlated with the general body weight of the fetus at that time, and nutritional deficiencies at the time of either brain growth spurt may produce deficiencies of brain growth and intelligence which can never be made up subsequently by adequate nutrition. Premature babies who are light for their gestational age are more likely to be mentally handicapped than those premature babies of normal weight for their gestational age. Full-term babies, too, who are light for their gestational age, run a higher risk of being mentally handicapped than those of normal birth weight.

A. NUTRITIONAL AMENTIA

From what has been said it will be clear that any nutritional deficiency, such as protein lack, which can cause retardation of general body growth may result in intellectual deficiency if it occurs at the time of the brain growth spurt. During intra-uterine life, placental insufficiency is an important cause of poor fetal growth. Placental insufficiency may be due to developmental abnormalities of the placenta or various maternal disorders, such as cardiovascular disease, repeated antenatal haemorrhages, chronic renal disease, toxaemia of pregnancy or severe diabetes mellitus. In the latter, fetal hypoglycaemia, induced by treatment of the maternal diabetes, may be an additional adverse influence on fetal development. Smoking during pregnancy causes fetal underdevelopment, partly by causing vasoconstriction and reduced placental blood flow and hypoxia, and partly by depleting the maternal stores of vitamin B_{12}, upon which the fetus makes heavy demands for its normal development.

Excessive alcohol consumption during pregnancy (either steady or binge drinking) can lead to fetal abnormality. As well as mental handicap, a number of physical abnormalities may ensue. These include short palpebral fissures, epicanthic folds, microcephaly, cardiac septal defects and joint anomalies. It is probably wise to advise pregnant women to avoid alcohol altogether.

There is a greater risk of underdevelopment in multiple than in single pregnancies.

Low maternal urinary oestriol excretion is an important indication of retarded fetal growth. Early recognition of retarded fetal growth and, if possible, the treatment of its cause or the correction of postnatal dietary deficiencies before the period of brain growth spurt ends, may avoid any impairment of intelligence.

1. Neonatal Hypoglycaemia

Babies who are light for their gestational age are particularly likely to develop hypoglycaemia, due to their poor stores of glycogen in the liver. Where the blood glucose level is allowed to remain below 20 mg/100 ml death may occur, or permanent brain damage and mental handicap may result. The signs of neonatal hypoglycaemia include a poor sucking reflex, apnoeic attacks, convulsions, restlessness and abnormal sensitivity to auditory and tactile stimuli, to which the baby responds with widespread tremors.

To reduce the risk of permanent brain damage, the acute symptoms are treated by intravenous transfusion of glucose, perhaps with hydrocortisone injections, until the blood glucose level has remained above 20 mg/100 ml for 12 hours.

2. Anoxia

The human brain is capable of surviving deprivation of oxygen for only very short periods and the brain of the fetus is very sensitive to anoxia. Anoxia may arise during pregnancy, due to placental insufficiency associated with developmental abnormalities, pre-eclamptic toxaemia or retroplacental haemorrhage. It may arise at birth, due to interference with the circulation by a prolonged second stage of labour or prolapse of the umbilical cord. Neonatal anoxia may be the result of depression of the baby's respiratory centre by heavy maternal sedation. Babies of low birth weight for their gestational age are particularly prone to the effects of anoxia and are likely also to be hypoglycaemic, due to their heavy demand on liver glycogen stores. Any severe respiratory infection in early childhood, before the brain growth spurt is complete, may cause anoxic brain damage.

B. AMENTIA DUE TO INFECTION

1. *MATERNAL INFECTIONS*

a. Due to Viruses

These are most likely to interfere with development of the fetus when they occur during the first 3 months of pregnancy, as in the case of rubella.

i. *Rubella (German Measles)*

The risk has been estimated as 60 per cent if the mother contracts rubella 3–4 weeks after the onset of her last menstrual period, as 35 per cent at 5–8 weeks, as 15 per cent at 9–12 weeks and as 7 per cent at 13–16 weeks, with an overall risk up to 16 weeks of 21 per cent. Maternal rubella without a rash or subclinical maternal rubella can also cause serious fetal damage. Subclinical infection is more likely in women who are reinfected after a vaccine-induced immunity than in those with a disease-induced immunity.

Affected children are usually microcephalic, with abnormalities of the eyes such as microphthalmia, cataracts, glaucoma or retinitis pigmentosa, and they may be deaf and have congenital heart defects. Their growth is frequently retarded, and shortly after birth they may suffer from thrombocytopenic purpura and hepatitis, both of which usually resolve spontaneously. The degree of mental handicap varies from severe, in the case of early maternal infections, to mild, in the case of later infections. It may be associated with speech disorders or autistic behaviour.

Dermatoglyphics show a significantly increased incidence of whorl patterns on the finger-tips and of simian creases or the so-called 'Sydney line' (which is formed by the extension of the proximal transverse palmar crease to the ulnar border of the hand). The risk of serious fetal complications of maternal rubella may be considered sufficient to justify termination of pregnancy, if the mother wishes this. It is hoped to reduce the incidence of congenital rubella by vaccinating adolescent schoolgirls and non-pregnant women, who lack rubella antibodies, with attenuated living viruses.

Although most attention has been focused on maternal rubella, evidence is accumulating of the possible importance of other virus infections during the first 3 months of pregnancy as causes of mental handicap, although they cause less severe congenital abnormalities. These include infections with cytomegalovirus, varicella (chicken pox), herpes simplex, infectious hepatitis, influenza A virus, mumps virus and poliomyelitis virus.

ii. *Cytomegalovirus Infection*

Evidence is accumulating that maternal cytomegalovirus infection may be responsible for far more cases of amentia in the offspring than maternal rubella.

As in the case of rubella, the fetus is more likely to be affected when maternal infection occurs early in pregnancy, but, in contrast to maternal rubella, the fetus may be infected late in pregnancy and the overall risk of 50 per cent is higher than in the case of rubella. The maternal infection is usually subclinical and unrecognized.

Affected children are born prematurely, with breathing difficulties, jaundice, hepatosplenomegaly and thrombocytopenic purpura. Many die within a few days of birth. Those that survive are usually microcephalic, with chorioretinitis, and may later develop infantile spasms or epilepsy and cerebral palsy and show varying degrees of mental handicap.

Dermatoglyphics: as in the case of congenital rubella there is an increased frequency of whorl patterns on the finger tips and of Sydney lines on the palms.

iii. *Varicella (Chicken Pox)*

Congenital abnormalities which have been reported after maternal varicella during the first trimester of pregnancy include limb deformities and the presence of skin scars along the length of the hypoplastic limb. The birth weight may be low and there may be feeding difficulties and failure to thrive, and chorioretinitis may be present and meningo-encephalitis may occur. As a result of the latter there may be brain damage and mental handicap.

b. Due to Other Organisms

i. *Syphilis*

This is fortunately a rare cause of amentia nowadays, but may take two main forms in the child:

CONGENITAL SYPHILIS

In this condition both mental and physical development may be obviously affected from birth, but usually the latter more than the former. The affected infant is anaemic and fails to thrive and may have a maculopapular skin rash. All organs of the body may be affected. Growth is stunted and the facial appearance is typical, with the so-called 'saddle-back' deformity of the nose, due to defective development of the bridge. Abnormalities of dentition occur, of which the most typical gives the upper central incisors a peg-shaped appearance, with a crescentic notch of the biting edge (Hutchinson's teeth). There are frequently developmental abnormalities of the eyes, including opacities of the cornea, strabismus and nystagmus. The central nervous system is affected to a variable degree and epilepsy may occur. The Wassermann reaction is not sufficiently constant in these cases for any diagnostic reliance to be placed on it.

JUVENILE TABOPARESIS

In this condition mental development may be normal until the age of about 9 or 10 years, when signs of adult taboparesis occur, with the characteristic disturbances of co-ordination and gait and spastic paralysis of the limbs. The reflex changes vary according to the relative involvement of the motor or sensory systems. Dementia occurs at first slowly, but progresses rapidly in the terminal stages and is accompanied by frequent epileptic fits. Death usually occurs within 10 years from the appearance of the first signs.

It may be possible to avert the progress of the disease with antibiotics, but the probabilities of normal mental development subsequently are extremely remote.

Positive Wassermann reactions in blood and cerebrospinal fluid occur more frequently than in congenital syphilis, and other characteristic changes occur in the cerebrospinal fluid, which gives a Lange gold curve of typical pattern.

ii. *Toxoplasmosis*

This is an infection by the protozoa *Toxoplasma gondii,* which is acquired from farm and domestic animals and which usually causes only mild symptoms in adult humans.

Serological evidence of infection at some time has been found in as many as 50 per cent of pregnant women in some country districts, but it is necessary for the primary infection of the mother to occur during pregnancy for the infection to be transmitted to the fetus. Transmission can occur throughout pregnancy, but the earlier the maternal infection the greater is the probability of fetal death and abortion. Where transmission occurs during the second half of pregnancy, the fetus may survive to term and show evidence of congenital infection at birth or this may not become apparent until the infant is several weeks old. The infection causes a severe encephalomyelitis, as a result of which either microcephaly or a mild hydrocephalus may occur, associated with various spastic deformities, convulsions and bilateral choroidoretinitis. Unilateral microphthalmia may occur. The liver and spleen are enlarged. Calcification of the scattered areas of brain damage may be apparent in radiographs.

The degree of mental handicap will vary according to the severity of the brain damage.

The diagnosis can be confirmed by various serological tests.

2. CHILDHOOD INFECTIONS

a. Due to Viruses

Encephalitis

This may arise as a primary infection of the brain or as a rare complication of any of the common virus infections of children. In the latter case its occurrence is often unrelated to the severity of the primary infection or to the effects on the fetus of maternal infection with the same virus. In some cases recovery may be complete. In other cases there may be signs of residual brain damage: hemiplegia, ataxia, aphasia, choreiform or athetoid movements, convulsions and varying degrees of mental handicap. The effect on intelligence may be relatively slight compared with the great disturbance of behaviour and personality which may result. This may take the form of pathological lying, stealing, viciousness and sexual behaviour.

Acute encephalitis lethargica, which rarely occurs as a major epidemic, but which may occur sporadically at any time, may cause amentia.

In amentia due to encephalitis lethargica, as in that due to meningitis, the impairment of intelligence may be less marked than the resulting personality change. However, encephalitis lethargica may damage the ganglia at the base of the brain sufficiently to produce post-encephalitic Parkinsonism, sometimes after an interval of years. The main signs of this condition are a generalized slowing of the bodily movements due to increased muscular rigidity, which gives a characteristic 'cog-wheel' sensation on passive movement of the joints. The normal mobility of the facial expression becomes lost and excessive salivation may occur. There may be periodic painful involuntary spasms of the external muscles of the eyes, as a result of which they become turned upwards so that only the whites are visible ('oculogyric crises'). The associated movements of the arms and legs in walking are lost and there may be a pill-rolling tremor of the thumb and first finger. In some cases hemiparesis occurs.

There is no specific treatment, but drugs are available to reduce the muscular rigidity and excessive salivation. Attempts are being made to treat the symptoms by localized brain operations.

The patient's slowness of response and movement should not be taken as a measure of his intellectual capacity and it should never be forgotten that in many cases the patient's understanding of events around him is not grossly impaired. For this reason the greatest care should always be taken to avoid statements in his presence which might be hurtful or embarrassing to him.

A clear-cut history of preceding encephalitis is frequently absent in patients developing signs of post-encephalitic Parkinsonism, but the abnormal sensitivity of a number of cases of amentia to the extrapyramidal effects of various tranquillizing drugs suggests the possibility that their amentia may, in fact, be due to undiagnosed encephalitis.

VACCINE DAMAGE

Some cases of brain damage and mental handicap have occurred following immunization with pertussis vaccine and, in cases where this is thought to have happened, families have received compensation from the government, under the Vaccine Damage Payments Act 1979.

The risk of vaccine damage has been estimated at 1 in 54000 completed courses of immunization or 1 in 155000 injections and is thought to be highest where there is a family history of allergy or in children with infantile eczema.

b. **Due to other Organisms**

Meningitis

This may occur in an acute form in primary cerebrospinal meningitis or as a complication of generalized bacterial infections or in a chronic form in tuberculous meningitis. In each case, the underlying cortex may be damaged with resulting neurological abnormalities and mental handicap, or mainly a personality change, as in some cases of encephalitis as mentioned above.

In some cases of meningitis, adhesions develop at the base of the brain which interfere with the circulation of cerebrospinal fluid and produce hydrocephalus, as a result of which the skull may be grossly enlarged in the characteristically globular fashion. There may be defects of vision and hearing and other signs of involvement of the central nervous system, depending upon the severity of the hydrocephalus.

The course of hydrocephalus is variable: it may progress rapidly to death in a short period or may develop slowly for a period until a balance between secretion and absorption of cerebrospinal fluid becomes established. During the stage of active development the fontanelles remain open and epileptic fits occur, but often cease later.

In all severe cases of hydrocephalus, cerebral atrophy occurs and there are severe amentia and wasting of the body, with spasticity of upper and lower limbs and eventual development of contractures. The patients are very prone to develop bed sores and, due to decalcification of their bones, spontaneous fractures frequently occur. The great weight of the head predisposes them to dislocation of the neck if unsupported during carrying. Death normally occurs owing to intercurrent infection of the chest or urinary tracts.

Attempts to find a drug to control the secretion of cerebrospinal fluid have so far proved unsuccessful, but it is possible to by-pass the site of the obstruction to the circulation of cerebrospinal fluid by providing a shunt between the ventricular and vascular systems by means of a Spitz–Holter or Pudenz valve, which allows a constant small volume of fluid to pass. If the flow is adjusted so that the ventricle is allowed to increase in size very slowly, the ependymal surface may become sufficient to absorb the net amount of fluid which cannot be absorbed through the normal channels. Unfortunately, the shunt systems are very prone to become infected and obstructed and have to be replaced periodically.

In childhood, any illness which produces dehydration, such as severe gastro-intestinal infection, may cause hypernatraemia and brain damage. In some of these cases, thrombosis of the venous sinuses draining the brain may occur and result in paralysis of the opposite side of the body, epilepsy and severe amentia. Severe brain damage and amentia may sometimes follow hyperpyrexia accompanying relatively trivial childhood infections such as tonsillitis or otitis media.

C. AMENTIA DUE TO TRAUMA

Direct violence during pregnancy is rarely a cause of amentia. A sufficient degree of violence to the mother to affect the fetus directly is more likely to cause a stillbirth. There are, however, various other physical influences to which the mother may be subjected which may prove sufficiently harmful to the developing fetus to result in amentia.

i. *Excessive Exposure to Radiation*

This may cause brain damage during the first trimester, whether it is the result of diagnostic X-ray examination of the lower abdomen or of atomic radiation, as in Hiroshima, where all 8 women survivors, who were within 1200 m of the atomic explosion and who were between the 7th and 15th week of pregnancy at the time, gave birth to microcephalic children. Other survivors have been found to have abnormal chromosomes which persist to this day. Exposure to excessive radiation may also produce mutation of genes, usually of recessive type, which may increase the probability that the members of subsequent generations may suffer from amentia. Present evidence suggests that the use of diagnostic ultrasound during pregnancy carries with it a far smaller risk of causing fetal abnormalities than diagnostic X-ray at that time.

ii. *Teratogenic Substances*

It is possible that substances used unsuccessfully to prevent conception or to induce abortion may yet damage the fertilized ovum sufficiently to cause congenital abnormalities and amentia in the offspring. There is, however, no definite evidence that either may be caused by hormonal pregnancy tests.

α. CAMPTOMELIC DWARFISM (SYNDROME OF MULTIPLE OSSEOUS DEFORMITIES)

In this syndrome the following congenital abnormalities are present: flat face, hypertelorism, micrognathia (small mouth), cleft palate and low-set ears. The scapulae, clavicles and ribs are hypoplastic. There is anterior bowing of the femora and tibiae, with a cutaneous dimple over the point of maximal deformity. The fibulae are hypoplastic and there is a talipes equinovarus deformity of the feet. A bilateral Sydney line may be present on the palms.

It is suggested that camptomelic dwarfism is caused by folic acid antagonists such as aminopterin or methotrexate, which are both used in the treatment of psoriasis and have a reputation as abortifacients.

Where the fully developed syndrome is present, the baby suffers from severe respiratory distress and dies in early infancy. Less severely affected babies may survive and are likely to be mentally handicapped.

Somewhat similar, but less severe, congenital abnormalities have been reported in the offspring of epileptic women taking anticonvulsants of the barbiturate and hydantoinate groups, both of which are known folic acid antagonists, during pregnancy. Affected children may be microcephalic, with hypertelorism, low-set ears, hare-lip and cleft palate, a short neck with a low posterior hairline and cardiac and minor skeletal abnormalities. A bilateral simian crease may be present, and mental handicap of varying degrees of severity.

Folic acid dietary supplements throughout pregnancy may reduce the incidence of these abnormalities.

Craniofacial malformations and abnormalities of the central nervous system have also been reported in the offspring of mothers who took tricyclic antidepressants during the first trimester of pregnancy.

β. ANENCEPHALY

In the complete form of anencephaly the brain may be entirely absent at birth, or absent except for the cerebellum and part of the basal ganglia, and is often associated with spina bifida. The condition is incompatible with survival. It is therefore not itself a significant cause of mental handicap, but it may be associated with other developmental abnormalities of the brain, possibly of related aetiology, occurring in later siblings. The cause of anencephaly is not known, but an increased incidence has been reported following epidemics of potato blight and it has been claimed that affected potatoes contain a substance which is teratogenic if ingested during pregnancy. These claims are, as yet, unproved and there is some evidence to suggest a genetic factor in that immigrants carry with them the incidence of their mother country.

Anencephaly may be diagnosed during pregnancy by ultrasound or by detecting abnormally high levels of α-fetoprotein in the amniotic fluid.

γ. RHESUS FACTOR INCOMPATIBILITY

The offspring of a woman with Rhesus-negative (Rh-negative) blood and a man with Rhesus-positive (Rh-positive) blood will have Rhesus-positive blood. The brain of the offspring may be damaged sufficiently to cause amentia as a result of the incompatibility between the mother's and the baby's blood. The mother starts to become immunized and to develop antibodies to the baby's blood during the first pregnancy, whether this continues to term or ends in either spontaneous or therapeutic abortion after the end of the first trimester. The child of the first conception is not usually affected, but later children are likely to be jaundiced at birth and subsequently to develop rigidity and athetosis due to damage to the basal ganglia by bile pigment ('kernicterus').

The development of antibodies and subsequent fetal damage may be prevented by injecting non-immunized Rhesus-negative women with anti-D γ-globulin within 48 hours of delivery. Where maternal immunization has already occurred and amniocentesis indicates a rising concentration of bilirubin due to destruction of fetal red blood cells, fetal damage may be reduced or prevented by injecting packed red blood cells into the fetal peritoneal cavity *in utero* or carrying out a complete exchange transfusion on the fetal blood *in utero*. Exchange transfusions may also be carried out immediately after birth if the condition has not previously been diagnosed. The necessity for exchange transfusions may be reduced by giving phenobarbitone to mothers during the last 2 weeks of pregnancy. It has been claimed that phototherapy of affected infants also reduces this necessity. Phenobarbitone and phototherapy may be effective also in reducing hyperbilirubinaemia and the risk of brain damage in premature or 'light-for-dates' babies or due to drugs such as long-acting sulphonamides taken late in pregnancy.

It has been suggested that Rhesus factor incompatibility may cause damage *in utero* and amentia, even when there is no motor involvement or history of jaundice at birth, and it has been reported that the incidence of Rhesus-negative blood is twice as high in the mothers of the mentally handicapped as in mothers of normal children.

iii. *Precipitate Labour*

When the second stage of labour is too rapid for proper moulding of the baby's head to take place, the brain may be damaged either directly or as the result of haemorrhage due to the tearing of the cerebral blood vessels. The damage is usually unilateral, with hemiplegia on the opposite side of the body and a high incidence of epilepsy and varying degrees of amentia. In some cases, hydrocephalus may result from obstruction to the circulation of cerebrospinal fluid by adhesions following haemorrhage at the base of the brain. The condition has to be distinguished from congenital diplegia of intra-uterine origin, which is the result of excessive exposure to radiation, intra-uterine infections, anoxia or nutritional defects. In these cases there is often a history of an easy birth of normal duration, with symmetrical spastic paralysis, athetosis or chorea and amentia, but with epilepsy an uncommon sequel.

iv. *Cerebral Trauma in Childhood*

Among the most tragic cases of amentia are those following accidental external violence to the skull in children of previously normal intelligence. The brain may also be damaged by multiple capillary haemorrhages which sometimes occur as a result of increased intra-cranial pressure during severe and prolonged bouts of coughing in whooping cough.

D. AMENTIA DUE TO POISONOUS SUBSTANCES

The developing brain may also be damaged by the ingestion of various poisonous metallic substances such as lead, copper, manganese and strontium. Lead poisoning occurs most frequently between the ages of 18 months and 3 years in children who live in poor urban areas and suck or chew lead-containing paints crumbling from the walls of old houses. It may also arise from the inhalation of lead from motor vehicle exhaust fumes. In the most serious cases, lead encephalopathy occurs with blindness, deafness, convulsions and severe amentia. In less severe cases, affected children tend to be withdrawn, irritable and disobedient and to show some autistic features or periodic psychotic behaviour. They may develop polyneuritis and optic atrophy. In all cases, the level of lead in the blood is increased and anaemia occurs with abnormalities in both red and white cells. Lead lines may be seen in X-rays of the bones.

The degree of brain damage may be reduced by facilitating the excretion of lead from the body in a non-toxic form by giving calcium versenate intravenously to severe cases or D-penicillamine orally to milder cases in older children and adults.

It is possible that mental handicap may result from brain damage due to methaemoglobinaemia caused by the ingestion of spinach with a high nitrite content due to incorrect preparation.

E. ISOLATION AMENTIA

The mind requires an external stimulus for its proper development, as do the muscles and bones, and it normally obtains this through the sense organs. If any of these organs are defective in their functioning, disturbance of perception, upon which all higher thought processes are built, is inevitable and in extreme cases, if this is not recognized and appropriate treatment and training given, various degrees of amentia may result. Hence the vital necessity of adequate physical examination of all cases of suspected mental handicap as early as possible to exclude the presence of any sensory defect such as high frequency deafness, which may interfere with the normal development of speech and masquerade as mental handicap. However, there is evidence that even when no sensory defect exists, enforced isolation for prolonged periods during the period of normal development, may produce amentia, as in the case of Kasper Hauser who, it is claimed, was kept in isolation in a small dark cell for the first 16 years of his life.

F. PARENTAL REJECTION

It is sometimes suggested that parental rejection is a primary cause of mental handicap. In the author's view, where rejection occurs, it is, in the vast majority of cases, a secondary result rather than a primary cause and develops out of the parents' frustration and disappointment at their inability to make a satisfactory relationship with the child due to its inherent mental handicap. Such parents frequently have a great sense of guilt and to add to it by suggesting they are primarily responsible for their child's condition is unforgivable.

The Abilities and Behaviour
of the Mentally Handicapped

The existence of the most severely mentally handicapped patient is merely vegetative. The patient is mute, completely helpless and lies in his cot showing no awareness of his surroundings, doubly incontinent, and throughout his life requires the same nursing attention as a small baby. With diminishing degrees of mental handicap, there is a progressive increase in spontaneous activity, which may include the ingestion of all manner of inedible objects ('pica') as well as the ability for self-care and the control of natural functions. A few words of speech emerge, but the grasp and understanding are very poor; at a lesser degree of mental handicap there is the ability to answer simple questions and obey simple commands, but not to initiate or maintain a conversation. In the middle range of severe mental handicap the latter ability is present, but the patient's thought processes are limited to the perceptual level, with no ability for conceptual thought and with marked defect of reasoning power. These patients are capable of simple routine work under close supervision, but left to themselves show little initiative or planning ability. They have poor powers of concentration. Some can read words of up to four or five letters and can write a letter from a copy, but cannot compose one unaided. Their general knowledge is often limited to that of their immediate surroundings and often they cannot give accurate information about their age, birthday or the present date, and cannot tell the time. They can count in a purely mechanical manner and, although they have some idea of relative money values, they cannot handle sums larger than about 20 to 30 pence.

At the upper limit of severe mental handicap patients can give personal information, know the date, tell the time and can often read quite fluently, but with very little grasp and understanding of the subject matter. They are able to compose and write their own stereotyped letters. The range of general knowledge is superficially good, but obviously defective on questioning. They are capable of such simple concepts as beauty and truth, although they may not always appear to be aware of the latter! They can do additions and subtractions, but fail on problems involving simple reasoning. They are, however, very easily led, and for this reason liable to be exploited either sexually or by unscrupulous employers or to be led into antisocial behaviour by undesirable acquaintances. It is these limitations which render them incapable of leading an independent existence.

The mentally handicapped are closely linked with the problem family group (the so-called 'submerged 10 per cent'), and with Lewis's subcultural group. These patients tend to breed true and to produce children with similar or lesser degrees of intellectual defect, whereas the severely mentally handicapped are more frequently born to parents of average or superior intelligence.

Although of normal appearance, and not grossly defective in ordinary school attainments, the mentally handicapped show no grasp of the principles which govern human behaviour. This is largely the result of their unstable background, in which parental immaturity and inconsistency in admonitions and punishments create confusion and insecurity in the child's mind which its own limitations of intelligence preclude it from resolving. It is not surprising, therefore, that it may rebel against the relative regimentation of school and tasks which it finds difficult, by truancy, seeking bad company and resorting to delinquency. Such individuals are hopelessly inadequate in a modern urban civilization and a number drift into crime and become repeated offenders: drunkenness, larceny, prostitution, neglect of children, indecent assaults, common assaults, arson, suicide and homicide, in that order of frequency.

It is possible to classify this group of individuals in the 'psychopathic disorder' category of the Mental Health Act 1983, and to call them 'mentally handicapped psychopaths'. The authors believe, however, that this practice is unhelpful to the mentally handicapped and is better avoided and that the term 'psychopath' should be confined to individuals whose behaviour disorders are not accompanied by subnormality of intelligence.

The mentally handicapped girl, so often deprived of affection in childhood, is apt to mistake sexual advances from the opposite sex for true affection, so that the incidence of illegitimate births in this group is high.

As might be expected, homosexual behaviour is apt to occur amongst mentally handicapped and severely mentally handicapped patients of both sexes as in any other community, but is less likely where mixing of the sexes is encouraged.

Mentally handicapped patients react badly to admission to hospital if brought into contact with the more severely mentally handicapped whom they sometimes exploit. The two groups of patients should therefore be treated in parts of the hospital remote from each other. The behaviour difficulties of the mentally handicapped patients are potentiated by their collection together in large groups, and it is desirable that they should be treated in wards for not more than 10–15 patients, staffed by most highly selected nurses with a proper understanding of the psychogenesis of their behaviour disorders. The success of such a ward, run as far as possible on permissive and psychotherapeutic lines, depends ultimately on the atmosphere of security, understanding and affection created by the nursing staff who, with the psychiatric staff, must inevitably act as parent substitutes towards the patients. It is therefore desirable that the same nursing staff should always work in the ward, as experience has shown that difficulties most frequently develop during the periods when patients are in the care of relief staff with whom they are unfamiliar.

The next stage in the rehabilitation of these patients presents a problem so far not satisfactorily resolved. Their need is for a stable home environment outside of hospital, but few have homes of their own to which they could be discharged with confidence. Neither local health authority hostels nor the majority of available lodgings are adequate substitutes for a real home, and, unfortunately, their choice of marriage partners is often unlikely to provide the stability they need.

Whatever the grade of mental handicap, a search should always be made for the cause of any misbehaviour. Even at the lowest level a simple cause will usually be found for a temper outburst in the behaviour of those in immediate contact with the patient. More severe temper outbursts may follow an epileptic fit or represent an epileptic equivalent or may be a manifestation of a psychotic illness. In higher grades it may be related to anxiety about relatives in the absence of letters or visits, jealousy of other patients or resentment of staff attitudes, or may be associated with premenstrual tension. A frequent cause of misbehaviour is a broken promise made to a patient by a relative or member of the staff. No definite promise should ever be made to a mentally handicapped person unless there is a reasonable prospect of its fulfilment. It is important that all staff should recognize these disturbances for what they are and should play their part in alleviating them rather than regarding them merely as aggravations and provocations to be endured and to be explained away simply as the sort of behaviour to be expected of the mentally handicapped, without any specific cause for them.

Serious, premeditated, planned violence is rare in the mentally handicapped and is likely to occur only in the least handicapped. When violence occurs in more mentally handicapped patients, it is usually an immediate response to provocation, similar to the reaction of a normal child of similar mental age, who has not yet learnt self-control.

However, in some severely mentally handicapped patients, impulsive, destructive, and aggressive behaviour occurs periodically and quite unpredictably, without any environmental cause. The management of these patients has been revolutionized in recent years by the use of first chloropromazine and then other phenothiazine derivative drugs and drugs such as haloperidol. Under the control of these drugs many patients become much more manageable and accessible to environmental influences, with great improvement in their behaviour and in the capacity for useful occupation. Since their introduction the necessity for seclusion or restraint has become less frequent, and life for patients and staff has become much more tolerable.

In choosing a drug to control disturbed behaviour it may be helpful to bear the following points in mind:

1. PHENOTHIAZINES

a. *DIMETHYL-AMINOPROPYL SIDE-CHAIN GROUP*

The predominant action of this group of drugs (which includes chlorpromazine, promazine and methotrimeprazine) is to inhibit behaviour to varying degrees. They also change the normal hypertensive effect of adrenaline to a hypotensive effect and should, therefore, be avoided when hypotensive drugs are being given.

The most widely used drug in this group is chlorpromazine, which may cause epileptic fits in up to 1 per cent of cases if the doses given are too large or increased too rapidly. Females on this drug are twice as likely as males to develop allergic rashes, angioneurotic oedema and photo-sensitivity, which disappear with reduced dosage and the administration of antihistamines. Prolonged administration of the drug in high dosage may cause permanent purplish-grey pigmentation on the exposed parts of the skin and a myriad of white dots in the anterior part of the lens capsule and in the cornea. Jaundice, due to intrahepatic obstruction of allergic origin, is more likely to occur in women than men and normally disappears in a few weeks without any residual ill-effects.

b. *PIPERAZINE SIDE-CHAIN GROUP*

This group of drugs (which includes fluphenazine, perphenazine, prochlorperazine, trifluoperazine, thioproperazine and thiopropazate) has a marked effect on the extrapyramidal system and may produce the signs of drug-induced Parkinsonism and various dystonic–dyskinetic reactions and akathisia, which may be very distressing to the patient and alarming to the onlooker. The milder extrapyramidal side-effects can usually be controlled with drugs such as orphenadrine (50–100 mg t.d.s.) or benztropine mesylate (1–4 mg b.d.). The dystonic–dyskinetic reactions may persist for several months after the phenothiazine has been stopped, but may respond to the administration of calcium tablets (1 tablet t.d.s.).

The inablity to sit still and the restless pacing up and down, which is characteristic of the patient with akathisia, is apt to be mistaken for the signs of anxiety and to lead to the administration of an increased dosage of the phenothiazine which has caused the condition. The treatment is to change to a non-phenothiazine derivative.

c. *PIPERIDINE SIDE-CHAIN GROUP*

This group of drugs (which includes thioridazine, pericyazine and pecazine) has less effect on the extrapyramidal system, but is more likely to produce leucopenic–agranulocytic complications, particularly in females over the age of 40.

2. NON-PHENOTHIAZINE TRANQUILLIZERS

Haloperidol, a butyrophenone derivative, is very effective is controlling overactivity in mentally handicapped patients, especially children, but occasionally has the opposite effect of increasing over-activity. It is apt to produce extrapyramidal side-effects which can usually be controlled easily with the drugs previously referred to. Claims have been made for the beneficial effects of some anticonvulsant drugs such as sulthiame, beclamide and carbamazine on disturbed behaviour in some non-epileptic mentally handicapped patients.

When a drug has been found to improve the behaviour of any mentally handicapped patient, it is very tempting to continue that drug indefinitely, but it should be a general rule to review its use periodically and, if it is not found possible to discontinue in at least temporarily, to ensure that the dose prescribed is the minimum which will produce the therapeutic effect desired. In all cases, it is essential that regular red and white blood counts are carried out if serious, and sometimes fatal, blood dyscrasias are to be avoided. In this connection, when treating anaemia, it should be remembered that the concurrent administration of ferrous sulphate and the tetracyclines by mouth results in a reduction of the plasma level of the latter to only 10–50 per cent of the level expected.

BEHAVIOURAL PROBLEMS

It is not surprising that some of the mentally handicapped, often with organic brain dysfunction and always with some difficulty in comprehending the world around them, present with behavioural problems. Sometimes these are exacerbated by inappropriate handling and it can be difficult for patients who may, quite wrongly, feel guilty at having a handicapped child, to provide the firmness and consistency needed by all children.

For this reason, whenever a child or indeed an adult, presents with disordered behaviour, it is important that time is taken with the family to understand something of the psychodynamics within it and to get details of exactly how the problem presents and how it is normally dealt with. In some cases the behaviour is directly attributable to organic brain damage or to superimposed psychiatric illness, in which event appropriate medication will be prescribed. Otherwise, an approach incorporating the principles of behaviour modification is of value.

BEHAVIOUR MODIFICATION

The principles used are simple, but the technique needs to be carefully thought out and the plan of treatment tailored to each individual. The basic principle is that desirable behaviour is rewarded and undesirable behaviour is ignored. Unfortunately, people frequently do the opposite, e.g. if a child is playing quietly it is left alone, but when it starts to scream or otherwise misbehaves, it is immediately rewarded by attention! In order to institute a programme of behaviour modification it is necessary to have good base line observations and, armed with these, it is frequently possible to draw up a plan. The plan must be followed consistently by all those in contact with the mentally handicapped person, at home, school, training centre, hospital ward and in all relevant departments. Following the general principles, it is possible often to effect considerable change, although there are certain limitations. There is clearly some behaviour which cannot be ignored completely and in that case, the response has to be as unrewarding and neutral as possible. In these situations, sometimes the 'time out' principle can be used, where the individual is placed in an unrewarding situation for a short time. This may be a quiet room or, sometimes, simply a quiet area in the corner of a room.

Another form of management, using behavioural principles, is the use of a token economy, whereby people 'earn' rewards or tokens which can be exchanged for specific treats. One other important principle in using behavioural techniques is that the reward which is chosen must really be seen as a reward by that individual, whether or not the staff consider it to be so! Sometimes the 'reward' may simply be the obvious approval by the staff or parents. It is worth remembering, however, that autistic children have been shown to react negatively to expressed affection and for them a more neutral response, accompanied by a physical reward such as a sweet, is more effective. For more detailed descriptions of behaviour modification specialized texts should be used.

Conditions Associated with Mental Handicap

AUTISM

Autism is a term which was first used by an American doctor named Kanner to describe children who had a particular difficulty in relating emotionally to people, although the condition had been recognized and described by many workers earlier. Kanner attributed the condition to emotional factors in the environment, but later work has shown that it is most likely to have an underlying organic neurological pathology, and it has been suggested that it is associated with dysfunction of the reticular activating system in the brain stem. There is considerable misunderstanding about the condition and parents sometimes welcome the diagnosis as implying that their child is in fact highly intelligent and will need help only to express this intelligence. The reverse is the case and in fact about 50 per cent of autistic children are severely mentally handicapped and only about 20 per cent are of normal intelligence. Even they may be very limited in achievement because of the social limitations which are an inherent part of the condition. Autism occurs about three times as often in boys and was originally thought to occur more frequently in higher social class families. This may have been a false supposition, resulting from the fact that the earliest cases described by American workers were in private practice.

The condition occurs usually in the first 18 months of life, although occasionally one sees the classical picture after an illness such as encephalitis in an older child. Frequently the mother is aware that 'something is wrong' before professionals who are consulted can find anything on objective examination. The following are the features of autism:

1. Failure to develop normal interpersonal relationships. The autistic baby shows a characteristic disinclination to cuddle and later tends to avoid direct gaze and shows an increasing withdrawal from social contacts secondary to

2. Difficulty in comprehending spoken and gesture language and in developing normal and gestural speech. This appears to be the primary disability in autism. Some autistic children never learn to speak. In others, the development of speech is delayed and is

75

characteristically echolalic, with immediate repetition of words just heard or constant repetition of words heard in the more remote past. Words tend to be confused with those of similar sounds or to be mispronounced, and the sequence of letters in words or of words in sentences to be muddled. Normal intonation is absent. Autistic children are late in learning to point at objects and do so in a vague, imprecise way. They do not learn to make use of mime or facial gesture themselves in communication or understand its use by others.

3. Rigid patterns of behaviour with strong resistance to change. Autistic children show rigid patterns of behaviour which they carry out with ritualistic fervour, and include abnormal attachment to favourite objects such as a tin lid, a shoelace or cup. Any attempt to alter the pattern of behaviour or to separate an autistic child from his favourite object may produce a violent emotional reaction or outburst of temper. A similar outburst may be precipitated by the presence of a particular everyday object or some rearrangement of objects in their environment from their normal, familiar pattern. In these episodes, an autistic child may become aggressive or may inflict injuries on himself by biting his hands or wrists. When less excited, the child may carry out various stereotyped movements such as flicking his fingers in front of his eyes, flapping his hands, grimacing, jumping up and down or walking on tip-toes. In addition to their speech problems, autistic children have difficulties in understanding their visual perceptions and as a result tend to prefer to explore their environment by touching, tasting and smelling objects around them. They may also confuse right and left, up and down and may find it very difficult to copy skilled movements made by others.

There is no specific treatment for autism, but tranquillizers may be useful in reducing overactivity, and claims have been made for the beneficial effects of operant conditioning (behaviour modification) in helping autistic children to acquire specific skills and to modify their disturbed behaviour. The prognosis is best in children with IQs over 60. However, there is no evidence that for equal expenditure of time and manpower the prognosis in the case of autistic children is better than that of non-autistic children of similar IQ.

Autism should not be confused with specific developmental dyslexia, in which impaired language development occurs in the form of a specific delay in learning to read and spell, in association with otherwise high general intelligence and stable behaviour. As in autism, the incidence is higher in boys than in girls and there is difficulty in distinguishing left from right, and probably an underlying genetically determined neurological lesion.

COMMUNICATION DIFFICULTIES

SENSORY DEFECTS

Mental handicap may be accompanied by defects of sight or hearing, either as a further manifestation of faulty fetal development or as an acquired handicap. In either case it is important that the associated condition is diagnosed and, where possible, treated. People who already have intellectual difficulty in understanding the world around them need their other senses to function as well as possible, so the prescription of glasses or hearing aids is even more and not less important than in other members of society.

It is helpful to have specialized units where people with similar handicaps can be trained and live together. In such units the buildings can be adapted to provide specific help. For example, units for the partially sighted can have especially good lighting and walls with various tactile surface finishes to help the residents find their way round.

It is important that such sensory defects should not be overlooked as they often suggest a more severe degree of mental handicap than in fact exists and for this reason, whenever their presence is suspected, expert advice is sought from the ENT and ophthalmic specialist.

Sometimes the mentally handicapped do not acquire speech even when their comprehension is quite good and the hearing and speech apparatus appear to be normal. In these cases the help of a speech therapist is required, who may teach 'signing' as an alternative means of communication. The most commonly used method is MAKATON, which is essentially a miming sign language and should be used together with the spoken word by the teacher. Parents sometimes express anxiety that their child, if taught, will use signs rather than develop speech, but in fact if the two are used together it is sometimes possible to encourage the use of spoken language as the individual develops greater confidence in communication.

EPILEPSY IN THE MENTALLY HANDICAPPED

Epilepsy is a condition characterized by abnormal electrical discharges in the brain and with a variety of clinical manifestations. It can be of unknown origin (idiopathic) or can result from organic changes in part of the cerebral cortex. This being so, it is not surprising, bearing in mind that mental handicap is also caused by damaged or abnormally functioning brain, that the two conditions frequently occur together.

Convulsions in newborn babies may be due either to metabolic disorders or to brain damage. The latter, which tend to occur in the first 3 days of life or after the 8th day, have a worse prognosis than the former, which tend to occur between the 5th and the 8th day. Of particularly serious prognosis as regards progressive mental deterioration, dementia and severe degrees of mental handicap are the 'infantile spasms' (or 'salaam' spasms) in the 1st year of life, in which the child suddenly falls forwards and prostrates itself in the prone position. Such attacks are associated with a characteristic pattern in the EEG called 'hypsarrhythmia', but this EEG abnormality may be present with a similarly serious prognosis without the presence of salaam spasms. Hypsarrhythmia may result from a variety of causes of brain damage, including hypersensitivity to immunization in infancy against various diseases. The hypsarrhythmic pattern may be abolished by the administration of cortisone, but the prognosis as regards normal mental development remains bad, being relatively better when infantile spasms are absent initially.

In the so-called 'Lennox syndrome' there is progressive mental deterioration, starting between the ages of 1 and 6 years. Two types of seizure occur: one similar to petit mal and the other, in which a sudden tonic, but never clonic, seizure affects the limbs. The EEG abnormalities are distinctive from those in hypsarrhythmia and true petit mal. The seizures in Lennox syndrome do not respond to the usual drugs used in the treatment of grand mal and petit mal, but they are said to respond to diazepam.

Many children have convulsions when they have a fever of whatever cause, known as febrile convulsions. Typically, these occur while the temperature is rising and last under 10 minutes. In two out of three cases it is a once only occurrence, but if they last longer than 15 minutes or are followed by a transitory loss of power of one side of the body—Todd's paralysis—they are more likely to indicate that the child will develop epilepsy and need anticonvulsant medication.

The main forms of epilepsy are:

Generalized, with loss
  of consciousness
    { Grand mal, which is the commonest
     Petit mal (or 'absences')

Partial, with clouding
  of consciousness.
    { Focal (temporal lobe)

The same patient may have more than one form.

GRAND MAL FITS

The classical grand mal seizure has three distinct phases, sometimes preceded by an 'aura' or sensation that the fit is about to occur. There may also be a prodromal period, which may last for several days, when the patient's behaviour is unusual in some way and this may be a warning of an impending fit to those who are familiar with him.

Tonic: The patient falls to the ground, sometimes emitting a cry, the breath is held and he becomes blue due to lack of oxygen.

Clonic: Regular jerking movements of the limbs occur, frequently accompanied by frothing of the saliva. Urine may be voided.

Recovery: The movements stop and the patient is initially confused and drowsy.

After a major fit, the individual may complain of headache or want to sleep, although frequently, after a brief period of confusion, he resumes normal activities.

The management of a major fit is simple. The patient should be turned onto the right side, clothing loosened and precaution taken that he does not injure himself, for example, by knocking against a hard object. It is not necessary to try to put a gag in the mouth, as this can increase the likelihood of injury to the tongue or damage to the teeth.

PETIT MAL FITS

These are attacks of short duration, characterized by a brief vacant period lasting only a few seconds, which may be missed or misdiagnosed as 'lack of attention'. The diagnosis can be confirmed by the presence of a characteristic electroencephalogram.

COMPLEX PARTIAL (TEMPORAL LOBE) FITS

These can be difficult to diagnose and may be manifested as periods of unstable behaviour or episodes of apparently purposeful 'strange' behaviour, sometimes accompanied by lip smacking. Again, the diagnosis can sometimes be confirmed by demonstrating an abnormal pattern in the temporal lobe on electroencephalography. If such an abnormality is not manifest, the diagnosis can still be made on clinical observation.

Myoclonic epilepsy, in which involuntary jerking of a limb without loss of consciousness is a manifestation of cerebral dysrhythmia, is a fairly common accompaniment of those cases of severe mental handicap due to encephalitis or meningitis.

Epileptic attacks can be precipitated by stress or by physical conditions such as constipation or illness and are sometimes more frequent in females at the time of menstruation.

DRUGS

For many years phenobarbitone was the most commonly used anticonvulsant, but it has now largely been superseded by newer drugs, which are less likely to cause depression or irritability.

The drugs now most commonly used are:

Grand Mal: Sodium Valproate (Epilim); Carbamazepine
(Tegretol) and Phenytoin (Epanutin)
Petit Mal: Sodium Valproate; Ethosuximide; Carbamazepine

As far as possible, fits should be controlled with one drug. With polypharmacy, drug interactions are likely to occur and accurate monitoring is more difficult. However, some difficult-to-control epileptics can be controlled by adding small doses of clobazam to another anticonvulsant. It is not usually effective on its own. Occasionally, a major fit does not finish spontaneously or the patient may have a rapid succession of fits without fully recovering between them. This is known as 'status epilepticus' and requires medical intervention, frequently with intravenous diazepam, although in young children rectal diazepam may be effective and is more easily administered.

Phenytoin may produce toxic effects, particularly in children, when the plasma level exceeds 35 μg/ml. The most common are cerebellar ataxia and nystagmus, a morbilliform rash and gum hypertrophy, which may require surgical excision by a dental surgeon. High plasma levels of phenytoin are more likely to occur when other drugs such as sulthiame and diazepam are given concurrently.

All anticonvulsant drugs tend to lower the serum folate level, with the risk of producing mental deterioration, but combinations of anti-convulsants are worse than single drugs. Administration of folic acid alone may produce an increase in the frequency of fits and a fall in the serum vitamin B_{12} level, which if untreated may result in subacute combined degeneration of the spinal cord. This does not happen if folic acid and vitamin B_{12} are given together. Doses of folic acid, 5 mg once a week, and of vitamin B_{12}, 250 μg once a month, are effective in preventing mental deterioration when given as soon as a patient is put on anticonvulsant drugs. The dosage of either may have to be increased in established cases to correct the abnormal serum levels. Yeast tablets at the rate of 3 a day may prove equally effective in preventing both folate and vitamin B_{12} deficiency at very much less cost.

It is important that care staff, in whatever setting, keep a record of fits and that serum levels of anticonvulsants are monitored so that medication can be changed when necessary. Some people eventually outgrow their epilepsy and in that case it may be possible eventually to stop medication completely.

HYPERKINETIC SYNDROME

This syndrome which occurs in childhood in boys more often than girls, may be the result of brain damage due to a number of different causes. Its onset is at any time between a month and 3 years (average 18 months) after the damage.

The cardinal sign of this syndrome is, as the name implies, excessive motor activity. The child is never at rest, often by night as well as by day. Its activity is not directed to any useful purpose and often takes the form of destructiveness and viciousness towards other children. The child's concentration is very poor, the child is easily distracted and there is no ability for sustained affection. The mood fluctuates against a background of euphoria and the child shows a lack of shyness and fear. In addition to mental handicap, there may be associated epileptic fits or EEG abnormalities without fits. Barbiturates are contra-indicated as they may aggravate the overactivity and carbamazepine is usually the anti-convulsant of choice.

Treatment of the condition consists of general management, using the principles of behaviour modification, and sometimes drugs are helpful. Some children respond to tranquillizers, and haloperidol has been found to be particularly helpful, although the dose has to be carefully monitored to minimize side effects. Paradoxically, in some cases, hyperactivity is reduced by treatment with amphetamines or certain antidepressants, possibly due to the stimulation of the cortical controlling centres. Recently pyridoxine (vitamin B_6) has been reported to be of value and is certainly worth trying as it is non-toxic and being water soluble is readily excreted.

There has also been interest during the past decade in the possibility of sensitivity to particular foods being implicated in the aetiology of hyperkinesis and a number of diets, such as the Feingold, have been tried. The Feingold diet avoids artificial additives, while others avoid cereals or other specific foods. The evidence is not statistically convincing but, if parents are keen to try such an approach, then they should be given any information they require. There is nothing to lose and possibly something to gain.

When the brain damage is less severe, the child's general overactivity may be less obvious, but he is characteristically awkward and excessively clumsy when tying his shoes, catching a ball or learning to ride a bicycle. He may show motor impersistence and be unable to maintain voluntary movements, such as keeping his eyes closed, fixing his gaze in a lateral direction, keeping his mouth open, or protruding his tongue.

The brain-damaged child may also have disorders of perception, such as disturbance of spatial relationships, concept of body-image and right–left orientation.

Generally, hyperkinesis reduces as the child gets older and simply to be able to give this reassurance to parents can be extremely helpful to them in coping with a child who has this very difficult to handle and exhausting condition. It is also important for the health and well-being of the whole family to build in periods of respite care.

SPASTICITY

Cerebral palsy may exist with or without associated mental handicap. It is caused by dysfunction of the motor parts of the brain. It is sometimes accompanied by choreo-athetosis, which indicates that deeper structures of the brain have also been damaged.

It is important that physiotherapy is available to help to prevent secondary deformities and to attain maximum function, but sometimes surgery becomes necessary. This is particularly so in cases of severe spasm of the adductor muscles causing scissor deformity of the legs, which can be released by cutting the relevant muscle tendons. The speech therapist may play an important part in training the patient to overcome difficulties in chewing and swallowing which are common accompaniments of spasticity. Baclofen is a useful drug in reducing spasticity and improving function. The dose has to be monitored carefully and tailored to the needs of each individual. The effect of too high a dose is to produce hypotonicity of the muscles but it is sometimes necessary to proceed to this dose first and then to reduce it to the optimum therapeutic level.

SUPERIMPOSED PSYCHIATRIC ILLNESS

There still exists in many people's minds confusion between mental illness and mental handicap. The two however are not mutually exclusive. Indeed, the mentally handicapped have a greater susceptibility to psychiatric illness than the rest of the population. The presentation of these illnesses is influenced, however, by the associated mental handicap. It was formerly thought that only people with mild mental handicap were likely to suffer from superimposed psychiatric illness but, in fact, with increasing awareness of the differing presentation of illness, it is realised that even quite severely mentally handicapped people can have a treatable psychiatric illness.

A. PSYCHOSES

1. *SCHIZOPHRENIA*

Schizophrenia is most easily diagnosed in the mildly mentally handicapped, although it can occur in others. The diagnosis depends more on the observations of others than, as in the rest of the population, on subjective reports. The patient may be seen to be laughing or talking to himself or appear to be looking at what are presumed to be visual hallucinations. The level of functioning deteriorates and the patient becomes generally less accessible.

Hallucinations tend to be simple, very often consisting of hearing his name called, and delusions are similarly less complex and frequently of a paranoid nature. The treatment is with phenothiazines, although the dose is frequently less than that usually needed in the general population. Indeed, they should be used with caution as the mentally handicapped have an increased susceptibility to extrapyramidal side effects. Down's syndrome patients sometimes display a schizoid reaction, clinically similar to schizophrenia but with a better prognosis.

2. MANIA AND DEPRESSION

As in the rest of the population, the mentally handicapped may suffer from mania or depression, either episodically as features of an unipolar illness or as swings in a bipolar illness. There may be a positive family history but the presentation of the illness is affected by the lower intelligence.

The lower the I.Q. the less typical is the illness and, in those of lowest ability, it may only be guessed at by the episodic nature of certain behaviour disorders.

a. Mania

The presentation of mania is similar whatever the I.Q. The individual is overactive, talkative and needs little sleep. However, the mentally handicapped, not surprisingly, do not show the more subtle variations of speech, such as punning or rhyming, but may show flight of ideas or clang associations. They may be excessively jolly or, a more difficult symptom to manage, excessively irritable. A common complaint is that they keep the family awake at night playing their records. Mania is treated with the major tranquillizers. Phenothiazines, particularly chlorpromazine, can be used but the drug of choice is haloperidol. Lithium carbonate is also of great value in the treatment of mania and can be used either on its own or with tranquillizers. In cases of recurrent illness it can be given as long term prophylaxis.

Before a patient starts taking lithium, thyroid function tests should be done and, during treatment, repeated periodically as the drug can affect thyroid function. Blood levels of lithium need to be maintained within quite a narrow therapeutic range. Toxic side effects include nausea, vomiting, diarrhoea and tremor.

b. Depression

Again, the presentation of depression has some features common throughout the whole population, i.e. slowing of thought and behaviour, unhappy mood and weight loss. However, the mentally handicapped have certain differences in presentation. They tend to show regressed behaviour and may become incontinent or stop speaking, or may show considerable hypochondriacal obsessions with overlying behaviour of an hysterical nature. This can, unfortunately, sometimes be interpreted as simply 'attention seeking' or 'playing up' and the diagnosis of treatable depression missed.

The treatment of depression is mainly with the tricyclic or tetracyclic antidepressants. Amitriptylline is one of the most effective tricyclic drugs but, in the elderly, can cause urinary retention or cardiac toxicity. In these patients the tetracyclics should be used.

Occasionally, if a patient does not respond to drugs, it is necessary to give ECT which is particularly effective in the more severely depressed patients who are mentally retarded and deluded.

B. PSEUDO-PSYCHOSES

It is not uncommon for the mentally handicapped to describe in some detail and with considerable conviction, events which have no basis in fact. In some cases, the fantasies are of a harmless nature and are akin to those of small children, and in others, apparent delusions, as of pregnancy, are obvious attention-seeking devices. In some cases, such as those in which sexual interference by another person is alleged, this appears to be a wish-fulfilment fantasy when that person is an unattainable love-object or, conversely, an attempt to harm a person disliked by the patient. Such allegations are very distressing to the innocent victims of patients' attentions, but it is sometimes extremely difficult to establish their innocence in the face of patients' insistence on the truth of their statements and the absence of supporting or refuting evidence. Where such allegations concern an employer and are shown or admitted by the patient to be untrue, the possibility of the patient's future employment outside hospital may be prejudiced.

The sex chromosome abnormalities associated with mental handicap in both males and females are associated also with an increased liability to develop psychotic disorders.

C. NEUROSES

Although an acute anxiety state may appear in both mentally handicapped and severely mentally handicapped patients as an immediate response to a temporarily threatening situation, a chronic anxiety state, due to an unresolved conflict, is confined to the mentally handicapped and those at the upper end of the severely handicapped range. Similarly, reactive depressions are usually less severe and of shorter duration in the severely mentally handicapped than in those of higher intelligence.

Obsessional ruminations may appear secondarily in anxiety states and disappear when the underlying condition is resolved, but true obsessional-compulsive neurosis is a rare occurrence in mental handicap of any degree.

Conversion hysteria is not uncommon.

D. ORGANIC REACTION TYPES

As might be expected, the effects of any organic cerebral disease are more marked in the mentally handicapped than in the normal population. Thus, normal senile mental changes appear much earlier and progress more rapidly in the mentally handicapped, particularly in those with Down's syndrome.

Where congenital syphilitic infection has occurred, mental development may be arrested in childhood and be followed by the rapid dementia of juvenile general paralysis of the insane (juvenile GPI).

Acute confusional episodes may accompany intercurrent infections and generally disappear with the infection, but more prolonged confusion and mental slowing may be due to the toxic effect of drugs such as the anticonvulsants, or may be an indication of vitamin B_{12} or folic acid deficiency, which are by no means uncommon in the mentally handicapped receiving anticonvulsants for epilepsy. They may also be due to nicotinic acid deficiency, as part of the clinical picture of pellagra. Epilepsy itself is, of course, a cause of dementia.

PATTERNS OF SERVICE

Mental handicap includes a wide range of people with, as has been demonstrated, many aetiological factors and sometimes with associated physical or psychological handicaps. It is clear, therefore, that no single form of care will provide for these manifold needs. It is, however, important that a pattern of service is established to ensure that the needs of the mentally handicapped and their families will be met as far as possible and not depend on chance. Such a service will involve the integration of many disciplines and numerous agencies, which will probably have some lifelong involvement with the mentally handicapped person, but whose contributions will vary depending on the needs of the individual.

FAMILY NEEDS

When considering the needs of the mentally handicapped it is important to remember the needs of the family. Parents who have a mentally handicapped child have, in one sense, suffered a bereavement which may, however, be reactivated at various critical points throughout life (e.g. starting school, adolescence, leaving school). They have lost the normal child they were expecting and have to come to terms with quite a new and unplanned life style. They are likely to go through the well-recognized reactions of bereavement and almost all will benefit from psychiatric help in this process of adjustment. The authors believe that this can best be provided by the psychiatrist–specialist in mental handicap, who will also be involved in assessments, counselling and treatment of the mentally handicapped individual. The parents of even a very young child frequently have anxieties about the provision when he grows up, about the ultimate prognosis and, eventually, 'what will happen after we're gone'. It is important that they are allowed ample opportunity to express all these anxieties and to have their questions answered as fully and as honestly as possible. The earlier one makes a prediction of level of adult functioning the more likely one is to be wrong and it is important that the need for continued reassessments throughout life is made clear to parents. During the past decade there has been the increasing development of parent groups and this is to be welcomed and encouraged, particularly when such groups organize workshops and invite professionals to help them to greater knowledge and understanding. Without such professional support there is the possibility of parents reinforcing each other's anxieties or unrealistic hopes which can in the long run be unhelpful. As well as emotional help families will, of course, have many practical needs and sooner or later will require breaks from the strain of caring for their mentally handicapped members. This will be considered in detail later. Most mentally handicapped children now live at home and parental rejection at birth is now, fortunately, very rare. The care needed by a handicapped infant varies little from that of a normal child and the important work at this stage is the family psychiatry which lays down the foundations for acceptance of the handicap which will become increasingly obvious as the child grows older and fails to achieve normal developmental milestones.

The health visitor will visit the new baby, as in all families, but it is important to remember that the health visitor probably has very little experience of mental handicap and the community mental handicap nurse may have a great deal to offer at this stage. The parents may also now be introduced to other parents. The realization that they are not alone and the mutual support can be invaluable. The family doctor must be fully informed of any intervention from other agencies as he continues to have primary responsibility for the health of the family.

FINANCIAL BENEFITS

A number of financial benefits can be paid to the handicapped and the social worker involved with the family should ensure that all such benefits are claimed—some of these are:

NON-CONTRIBUTORY INVALIDITY PENSION (NCIP)

This is payable to anyone of working age when he has been incapable of working for 28 weeks. If a person is in institutional care it is paid at a reduced rate.

ATTENDANCE ALLOWANCE

This is available to anyone over the age of 2 years whose disability is such that they require continual or frequent supervision by day and/or night. It is paid at two rates—the day rate, which is lower, and the higher one, which is the 24 hour rate. The disability must have lasted 6 months before attendance allowance is payable.

MOBILITY ALLOWANCE

This is available to anyone aged between 5 and 65 years at the time of initial application whose ability to walk is very limited or whose health may be damaged by exertion. There are restrictions on the way this money can be spent.

SUPPLEMENTARY BENEFIT

This is paid at the normal or long term rate and it is sometimes advantageous to claim this benefit rather than NCIP.

Other benefits are available, but these are the most widely used.

DAY SERVICES

PRE-SCHOOL

Before reaching the normal school attendance age of 5 years, a number of alternative forms of support outside the home are available for the mentally handicapped child, depending on local provision and also the level and/or multiplicity of handicap. People frequently talk about how particularly important it is for 'education' to begin as soon as possible, but it is also essential to remember the importance of learning that happens at home and that the mother of a handicapped toddler herself has to continue to learn about her child. It is a more demanding and complex procedure than in the case of a normal child and a good parent-child relationship established then is invaluable later. A balance must therefore be found between encouraging stimulation from external sources and helping mother to feel comfortable and confident with her handicapped child, while also giving her the chance to have a break occasionally. There are a number of ways of achieving this:

1. *OPPORTUNITY GROUPS*

These operate with voluntary support and are attended by mothers with handicapped and non-handicapped toddlers. It is helpful if some of the volunteers, as is usually the case, have a relevant training.

2. *NURSERY SCHOOLS AND PLAY GROUPS*

Again, particularly in milder mental handicaps, these can be a way of integrating handicapped with normal children and introducing learning through play.

3. *PART-TIME EDUCATION AT SPECIAL SCHOOLS*

Special schools are encouraged, as space allows, to take mentally handicapped children from the age of two onwards, sometimes for part of a day.

4. INVOLVING FAMILIES IN SCHEMES SUCH AS PORTAGE

This means that families with guidance from professionals (who may for example be psychologists, community nurses or specialist social workers) learn systems of evaluation and goal-setting, thus gaining confidence as well as helping their handicapped child.

SCHOOL

Since the Education Act of 1971, the Local Education Authorities have had a statutory responsibility for providing education for the mentally handicapped which has been updated by the Education Act of 1981 and the Education (Special Educational Needs) Regulations 1983. This is provided in special schools catering for children with varying degrees of handicap.

In milder cases of handicap, or those without evident physical stigmata, the child may already have started attending a normal primary school before his inability to cope raises the possibility of mental handicap at which time, with the parents' consent, an educational psychologist is usually asked to complete an assessment. At this time also, the medical specialist may be involved in making the recommendation for transfer to a special school. The Education Act of 1981 makes it mandatory that all parents are given full reports about their children, both at this stage and annually thereafter. Schools usually provide a variety of classes for children of varying abilities and include special care classes for those who are profoundly or multiply handicapped, as well as special needs groups for hyperactive or behaviourally disturbed children. School continues compulsorily until the child is 16 years of age and may, if it is deemed advisable by a multidisciplinary assessment and with consultation with the parents, continue until the child is 19 years. This decision must be made on an individual basis. It is undoubtedly beneficial for many and capitalizes on the developmental spurt which often happens in the late teens. There are, however, some young people who develop better by moving on into the more grown-up world of the Adult Training Centre particularly when, as is usually the case now, this provides facilities for further education and literary skills as well as its other services.

The emphasis on all education of the mentally handicapped is to help them to acquire, as far as possible, the skills for everyday living: to dress and feed themselves, to help with simple tasks in the home and to learn about situations outside the home. These include shopping, road sense and, when possible, acquire simple literacy and numeracy. It is, however, more important for the mentally handicapped person to recognize various signs used socially such as those for ladies' and gents' toilets than to be able to read, without understanding, a Ladybird book!

ATCs (ADULT TRAINING CENTRES)

Adult Training Centres are provided by the local authority. The best of them provide genuine training and education as a continuation of that started at school, as well as special care and special needs units. The authors believe that it is also helpful to provide some work experience, such as that on a contract basis. In this way the mentally handicapped gain a sense of achievement and are not denied the dignity of doing a job.

For those who are more able, sheltered workshops of various kinds are available and in some of these an economic wage can be earned. This is a good preparation for employment in open industry, particularly if the trainees are taught the importance of good time-keeping and work habits and the significance of insurance cards, income tax and pension deductions and union membership etc.

EMPLOYMENT

With the current levels of unemployment in the country it is becoming increasingly difficult to find open employment for the mentally handicapped. However, some employers, having employed the mentally handicapped in the past and realizing that they can be particularly good employees, are willing to offer jobs. Generally speaking, these include such things as simple labouring, portering and cleaning and are suitable only for those with mild degrees of handicap.

ADOLESCENCE

Adolescence is a difficult time emotionally and the mentally handicapped are no exception. Sexual development with the accompanying endocrine, physical and emotional changes often causes particular anxiety in parents and in other care staff, particularly now that mixed residential accommodation is the rule rather than the exception. Simple sex education can be undertaken and SPOD (Association for Sexual & Personal Problems of the Disabled) based in London, produces helpful literature. Minor sex offences by the mentally handicapped are usually due to lack of understanding of what is expected as normal behaviour, rather than indicating any danger to the public. Mentally handicapped girls are vulnerable to sexual exploitation and particularly need education and guidance. Girls with Down's syndrome have a very low fertility, but it is a wise precaution to provide contraception for all mentally handicapped girls who may be sexually active, so as to avoid the possible emotional trauma of having their child taken into care if they are incapable of bringing it up themselves.

RESIDENTIAL CARE

CHILDREN

Nearly all mentally handicapped children now live at home, but most families require some respite from time to time and this is provided in a number of ways:

1. Short term fostering or family support schemes, where the handicapped child lives with another family for varying periods. The respite care family is paid a retainer as well as for each session of care provided.
2. Short term care in local authority homes, either those for non-handicapped children or, probably ideally, for those who are mentally handicapped. (Homes with non-handicapped children generally have residents with higher than normal levels of emotional disturbance and for this reason are not suitable to cater also for the mentally handicapped.)
3. Short term care in hospital—usually for the multiply handicapped or those who are, for a variety of reasons, difficult to manage.

ADULTS

As in the case of children, many adult mentally handicapped people now continue to live with their parents for many years. When this is no longer possible, a number of alternatives should be available, depending on the degree of independence which has been achieved. These may include:

1. Living independently, with supervision by social worker or community nurse.
2. Living with a family.
3. Minimal support unit, where a small number of handicapped people live together, again helped by regular visits from social worker or community nurse, both to ensure that no problems have arisen and to help with matters such as budgeting. (One of the factors which ensures the success of any residential unit in the community is that members have been fully assessed before going into it and have been chosen bearing in mind such factors as complementary skills and personality compatibility.) This is particularly relevant in smaller units, where personality clashes can be less easily absorbed than in larger units.
4. Staffed group home.
5. Hostels. Theoretically, hostels should be able to provide accommodation for the majority of mentally handicapped people who require residential staff, but unless staff ratios are adequate it is

found in practice that even quite minor behavioural problems can lead to a breakdown in the placement.

The number of hostels and family group homes for both sexes, provided by social service departments for mentally handicapped persons without satisfactory homes, but not requiring hospital care, is increasing but is still far short of what is required to ensure the proper placement of such persons. The same may be said of the provision by social service departments of accommodation for the short-term residential care of mentally handicapped persons living at home, during relatives' holidays or periods of sickness. Sometimes admission to hostels is preceded by a period of treatment and training in hospital. Some local authorities run sponsored lodgings schemes under which they subsidize the cost of keeping mentally handicapped people in approved lodgings.

LEISURE

All mentally handicapped people need access to leisure pursuits in order to have as full and enjoyable a life as possible. Unfortunately, they are not very good at designing or finding their own leisure activities and need some help. Groups can be organized to use some leisure facilities available to the general public, such as swimming baths or riding schools. It is also helpful, however, to have contacts with clubs such as the Gateway Clubs which are organized throughout the country for the mentally handicapped. Some, living in the community, also attend with considerable enjoyment various functions such as discos and concerts organized in mental handicap hospitals.

NON-STATUTORY SERVICES

Valuable contributions to community care are made by various non-statutory and voluntary organizations. Play groups are provided for preschool children, and baby-sitting services enable the parents to take a much-needed break from the care of their children. The principal voluntary organization concerned with the care of the mentally handicapped is the Royal Society for Mentally Handicapped Children (Mencap), which provides a wide range of facilities, both residential and non-residential, to supplement those at present provided by statutory authorities, while campaigning for the improvement of the quality and range of existing services by those authorities. The Spastics Society has for some years now recognized the mental handicap of many spastics and is providing education and residential care for them and, like Mencap, is actively campaigning with other voluntary organizations for improvement in existing statutory provision. The National Society for Autistic Children has similar aims for children with that specific disability.

Mind (The National Association for Mental Health), which pioneered courses for training teachers of mentally handicapped children and the staffs of adult training centres and hospital occupational therapy departments, now the responsibility of statutory authorities, continues to fulfil an invaluable role in organizing a wide range of courses and conferences for professional and lay members in the mental handicap field and in informing the general public of the needs of the service through its 'Mind' campaign.

Several non-statutory organizations provide long-term residential care for the mentally handicapped in village communities, such as the Camphill villages provided by the Rudolph Steiner Organization, the Home Farm Trust, the CARE villages and Ravenswood, a Jewish foundation in Berkshire.

THE ROLE OF THE HOSPITALS

The role of the mental handicap hospitals is changing for a number of reasons. First, there is an increasing, though still inadequate, development of alternative residential and training facilities in the community. Second, families are no longer so ashamed of having a mentally handicapped child and are, rightly, demanding that services develop locally. In the past the hospitals drew their populations from all over the country but the old days of large institutions being developed are gone.

This means that the hospitals which exist can offer a specialized service to their catchment areas. They are increasingly being used as resource centres and seen as a part of, rather than apart from, their surrounding communities. Before dealing with this aspect in more detail, it is important to remember that all the large hospitals in existence have many residents who will for a variety of reasons continue to live in them and that, although they will gradually reduce in size, the speed of this reduction is limited by factors other than the inherent ability of the residents or the willingness on the part of hospital consultants to discharge them. One may argue that this should not be so, but it is a fact. Hospitals will continue to need adequate resources to provide a good standard of life for those who will not move elsewhere, either because there is no place for them to go or because they themselves do not want to, as well as for those for whom hospital care is the most appropriate provision. For them, the hospital must provide a background of affection, security and stability, and facilities for the full utilization of such abilities as the patients may possess and for their recreational needs. Even some of the most severely mentally handicapped patients have their likes and dislikes of food, staff and companions, and deserve individual consideration. Wherever possible, the severely mentally handicapped patient with gross physical handicap should be got up and dressed each day and provided with toys to stimulate interest and activity. In the hospital for the mentally handicapped, more than any other, should the concept of the therapeutic community be implemented, for in such a hospital a majority of the patients will spend the greater part of their lives.

RESOURCE CENTRE

Over the years, the staff of mental handicap hospitals have acquired considerable expertise in handicap, which is now made available to the community in the catchment areas in the following ways:

ASSESSMENT

A full multidisciplinary assessment, either on a residential or day basis, is most important, both for the proper placement of the mentally handicapped and to ensure a full diagnosis with subsequent appropriate treatment. Even if a definite cause cannot be found, families very much appreciate a detailed assessment and gain considerable comfort from knowing that 'everything has been looked into'. It should be stressed that assessment will need to be repeated from time to time throughout life, particularly if difficulties arise.

MEDICAL CARE

On admission to hospital, the mentally handicapped patient is given a detailed clinical examination, with particular attention to the nervous system and sense organs, to exclude any specific sensory defect such as deafness or blindness. It is important that such sensory defects should not be overlooked as they often suggest a more severe degree of mental handicap than in fact exists, and for this reason, whenever their presence is suspected, expert advice is sought from the ENT and ophthalmic specialist.

X-ray, electro-encephalographic (EEG), air-encephalographic and pathological investigations are carried out as indicated by the clinical findings.

TREATMENT

Treatment, both of physical (including orthopaedic and dental) disabilities and of behavioural or psychiatric disorder, can be instituted. Where necessary, appropriate diets can be introduced. After the patient is discharged, it is important that he is followed up, both with his family and often with school, training centre or hostel, to ensure that treatment is understood and continued.

94

SHORT-TERM CARE. RESPITE CARE

Arrangements for respite care for families should be as simple as possible so that needs can be responded to quickly to provide:

1. Frequent regular stays to fit in with their needs as a family.
2. Regular, but infrequent, provision such as during school holidays, or only once a year when the rest of the family go away.
3. Occasional use when a particular need arises.
4. Crisis intervention.

The periods of respite care may vary between one day and one month or occasionally, in the case of family illness, even longer.

Generally speaking, hospital respite care is used for those mentally handicapped individuals who are either profoundly or multiply handicapped and who require a great deal of nursing care, or for those who have behavioural or psychiatric disorders. Sometimes, reassessment or changes of treatment are instituted during periods of respite care.

LONG-TERM CARE

The number of children admitted on a long-term basis to hospital is now negligible and, indeed, the number of adults so admitted is also reducing. Those who are admitted now are generally those needing intensive nursing care and medical treatment, either because of their degree of handicap or associated problems, physical, emotional or mental. This means that staff ratios will in the future need to be much higher than in the past.

MULTIDISCIPLINARY TEAM

In mental handicap, possibly more than any other branch of psychiatry, the multidisciplinary team is a reality and necessary for adequate assessment and treatment. Each member contributes his or her particular skills and, in the National Health Service, the consultant psychiatrist remains the person with overall responsibility for integrating the many disciplines concerned, and for ensuring the best possible treatment for the patient. All patients should be reviewed at regular case conferences attended by all disciplines, and patients themselves encouraged to participate in decision making.

One of the most gratifying and rewarding aspects of hospital care in recent years has been the development and expansion of the occupational therapy departments and the discovery of the previously unsuspected ability in simple handicrafts of patients with mental ages as low as 4 or 5 years. In the past, we have been too easily discouraged by the apparent hopelessness of these patients on an initial trial, and have regarded them as unemployable and allowed them to vegetate in the ward, with inevitable mental deterioration and behaviour problems. We now recognize that failure on the initial test is often not an adequate guide to true ability and that when taught useful crafts their behaviour can be improved and they do not deteriorate so rapidly. However, occupational therapy is very much more than handicrafts alone and embraces many other aspects of the patient's rehabilitation, social training, indoor and outdoor games, remedial gymnastics and outings to places of interest.

The authors believe that occupational therapy should be organized in departments separate from the wards and that it should be run by trained occupational therapists rather than by nursing staff, although it is important that student nurses should spend part of their training period in the department. There is no doubt that both patients and nursing staff of the wards benefit from their period of separation during the day. However, for those patients who are unsuitable for or unable to attend the occupational therapy department, occupational therapy groups are held on the wards by the nursing staff under the guidance of visiting occupational therapists.

In the past, a number of the less handicapped patients were employed initially in departments within the hospital before progressing to daily employment outside the hospital. The number of such patients has been considerably reduced as they have been transferred to residential accommodation in the community.

THE CONTRIBUTION OF VOLUNTEERS

Many hospitals have Leagues of Hospital Friends, the primary function of which is to befriend the patient who has no relatives or whose relatives take no interest in him. The Leagues' activities have been supplemented by those of a wide range of other voluntary groups, including senior school pupils and students, often co-ordinated by a Voluntary Services Organiser.

COMMUNITY TEAM

Community mental handicap teams have developed in slightly differing ways in different parts of the country, depending on local geographical and historical factors, but they always play an important part in maintaining the mentally handicapped in the community and frequently operate out from mental handicap hospitals.

The core members can be the psychiatrist, clinical psychologist and community nurse, all from the Health Service, and the social worker from the local authority.

OUT-PATIENTS

Out-patients may be seen in a hospital, a health centre, a school, training centre or any other suitable location and the authors have worked in all of these. Families may be seen at home, if they agree and if it is considered necessary. In every case, it is important that findings and recommendations are passed on, always, to the family doctor and, where appropriate, to other people who may be responsible for acting on them. (For example, a behaviour modification programme must include school or training centre as well as home, whether home is family or hostel.) Good communication is essential when such a complex network of people is involved.

Intelligence Tests

Intelligence tests are valuable aids in the assessment of the degree of mental handicap, but patients should not be classified on the evidence of intelligence tests alone, and attention should always be paid to their former history, including their school and employment record.

According to the psychologist Sir Francis Galton, a person is assumed to have a fund of general native intellectual ability which provides a background against which the more specialized native intellectual abilities operate. These specialized abilities include aptitudes in music, mathematics, creative ability, etc. All psychologists do not agree with Galton's views, but for our purposes they provide a useful working basis.

As will be seen later, some intelligence tests assess mainly general native intellectual ability, whereas others assess chiefly one or other of the specialized native abilities, and the results are dependent in part, at least, on a person's previous education. This ability to acquire knowledge and to profit by experience, however, is an important manifestation of a person's general native intellectual ability. Any test which will assess this general intellectual ability alone is of more assistance in the diagnosis of mental handicap than tests assessing specialized native intellectual abilities. We all know persons who have marked ability in a special direction whom we would regard as being far from intelligent generally.

The nature of a person's response on testing may provide valuable clues to the presence of brain damage and mental illness.

STANDARDIZATION OF INTELLIGENCE TESTS

Various tests were applied to large numbers of people of different ages and different classes and, from the marks they scored on each test, an average mark was calculated for each test at each age. That mark was taken as the normal for that particular age and tables were prepared showing the normal mark for each age. Anyone scoring a particular mark is said to have the mental age (MA) corresponding to the chronological age (CA) for which that mark is the normal. By dividing the MA by the person's chronological age and multiplying the result by 100 a percentage is obtained which is called the intelligence quotient or IQ of that individual. Because native intellectual ability is assumed for the purpose of intelligence tests to have reached the maximum by 15 years of age, in calculating the IQ the CA age is taken as 15 if the actual age exceeds this. (This does not mean that a person of 15 is as capable of forming sound judgements and of behaving as wisely as an older person, who has had the benefit of greater experience; but rather that the intellectual ability necessary to make best use of experience has normally fully developed by 15 years of age.)

Examples
Mental age 7½ years, chronological age 15 years:

$$IQ = \frac{MA}{CA} \times 100 = \frac{7\frac{1}{2}}{15} \times 100 = 50.$$

Mental age 6 years, chronological age 21 years:

$$IQ = \frac{MA}{CA} \times 100 = \frac{6}{15} \times 100 = 40.$$

It will be seen that a particular MA corresponds to a particular IQ at each CA up to 15 years. In practice, allowance is made in the tables over the age of 15 years for the falling off in some intellectual abilities which is a normal accompaniment of advancing age. However, nowadays IQs are computed by the more accurate deviation method, which does not involve consideration of MA and which makes an individual's IQs at different ages more strictly comparable.

If many persons are tested and a graph is prepared showing the percentage of the total gaining each IQ, the curve appears roughly as shown overleaf, with slightly more individuals at the lower end of the IQ range than at the upper end, due to the effect of non-genetic causes of impaired intelligence. If the distribution of intelligence depended entirely on genetic factors, the curve would be completely symmetrical about its mid-point, with the percentage of individuals with IQs less than 25 equal to that of individuals with IQs over 160.

About half the population have IQs within the range of 90 and 110. There is no sharp dividing line in terms of IQ between normal and subnormal intelligence, but current clinical practice sets the upper limits of mental handicap at about an IQ of 70 to 80, depending upon the particular test used. Equally, there is no sharp dividing line in terms of IQ between mental handicap and severe mental handicap. It must be stressed again, however, that in the present imperfect state of intelligence tests, the IQ cannot be regarded as a rigid criterion for the diagnosis of mental handicap or severe mental handicap.

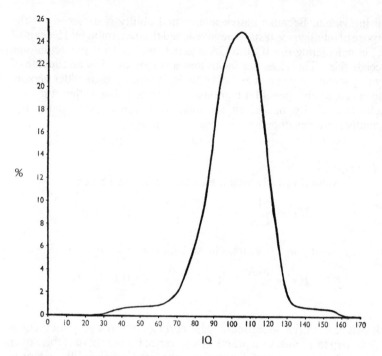

IQ

TYPES OF INTELLIGENCE TESTS

Intelligence tests as a whole may be divided into verbal and performance tests; but a particular battery of tests may assess both these aspects of intellectual ability.

Some of the tests are suitable for testing a number of persons at one time; this is referred to as 'group testing'; others can be applied only to individuals.

The tests in most general use at the present time are as follows:
1. Wechsler Intelligence Test.
2. Stanford–Binet Intelligence Test as revised by Terman–Merrill (Form L–M).
3. Raven's Matrices.
4. Porteus Maze.
5. Kent Oral Test.
6. Merrill–Palmer Test.
7. Drever–Collins Test.

1. WECHSLER INTELLIGENCE TEST

There are two separate scales in this test—the Wechsler Intelligence Scale for Children (WISC) for testing children between the ages of 5 and

15 years and the Wechsler Adult Intelligence Scale (WAIS) for testing persons between the ages of 10 and 60 years.

The Wechsler test is really a battery of tests, each of which has been shown from wide application to give reliable results. The complete battery consists of the following ten tests:

a. *INFORMATION TEST*

A person's score on this test obviously depends on his educational and cultural opportunities, and as such might not be considered to give a true indication of native intellectual ability. It has been found, however, that the range of a man's knowledge is usually a very good indication of his general native intellectual ability and is an indication of his alertness towards the world around him. It is, however, a poor test for those deprived of the opportunity of receiving verbal information.

A person's score declines less with age on this test than on any other test.

b. *COMPREHENSION TEST*

This may best be described as a test of common sense, which is a good reflection of general native intellectual ability. In addition, this test provides valuable clinical data about the subject, and a good indication of his personality may often be gained from the mode of his responses.

Persons who are unaccustomed to putting their ideas into words are handicapped on this test.

Scores on this test hold up well with age.

c. *ARITHMETICAL REASONING*

This test is an indication of a person's alertness, but it is obviously influenced by education and occupation and the result is affected by fluctuations of attention and by transient emotional reactions. Although dependent in part on specialized native intellectual ability, the results of this test are, in persons of mentally handicapped level at least, a good indication of general native intellectual ability.

Test scores fall with age.

d. *MEMORY SPAN FOR DIGITS*

This is a test of retentiveness, but a poor test of general native intellectual ability. However, like the previous test, it is good at the lower levels of intelligence and is helpful in picking out the severely mentally handicapped, who are often unable to repeat five digits forwards or three backwards.

This test may also reveal temperamental traits such as lack of attention or concentration.

Test scores fall rapidly with age.

e. SIMILARITIES TEST

This test provides a good indication of the logic of a person's thinking processes and is a very good indication of general native intellectual ability. The mentally handicapped may grasp superficial likeness, but they are usually quite unable to discern essential likeness.

In addition, the nature of the subject's responses may provide valuable indications as to his personality.

Test scores hold up fairly well with age.

f. PICTURE ARRANGEMENT TEST

This measures the subject's ability to comprehend and size up a total situation. The subject is required to rearrange a dissected comic strip so as to tell a story. Its value, therefore, varies according to the subject's interest in the content of the strip. It does, however, give a fair indication of a person's general native intellectual ability.

Test scores hold up badly with age.

g. PICTURE COMPLETION TEST

This measures an individual's basic ability to distinguish essential from inessential details.

The subject is required to name the part missing from an incomplete picture. The results depend in part on the subject's previous experience and familiarity with the picture presented, but this is a useful test at the lower end of the intelligence scale for indicating general native intellectual ability. It discriminates poorly, however, at higher levels of intelligence.

Test scores hold up well with age.

h. BLOCK DESIGN

This is the best of the Wechsler performance tests. It assesses the ability to recognize and reproduce designs and is an excellent test of general native intellectual ability.

The test is a modification of the Kohs block test.

Useful additional evidence of temperamental traits may be gleaned by watching the patient's attitude and emotional reactions while performing the test.

Test scores do not hold up well with age.

i. *DIGIT SYMBOL TEST*

This is a test of the subject's perceptual ability, but is also dependent on a manual factor. The subject is required to reproduce the unfamiliar symbols which are associated in the key with particular numerals. This test cannot, therefore, be used on illiterates who are not used to handling pencils and paper. In others, however, this manual factor is of importance in that the speed and accuracy with which the subject performs the test give a good indication of general native intellectual ability.

Test scores decline rapidly with age.

j. *OBJECT ASSEMBLY TEST*

This, also, is a test of perceptual ability and of the subject's reaction to the whole and of his ability to form a critical understanding of the relationship of the individual parts. The subject is required to piece together three sets to form a mannikin, a profile and a hand, but is not told the nature of the completed object before the test.

This is more a qualitative test of the subject's thinking and working habits than a reliable quantitative test of general native intellectual ability.

VOCABULARY TEST

This serves as an alternative test. Contrary to general belief, the size of one's vocabulary is an excellent indication of one's general native intellectual ability as well as being an index of one's education, and serves as a measure of one's learning ability.

Test scores hold up better than those on most other tests in the battery, but do fall off somewhat with age.

The complete battery of tests may be given or, if time does not permit, the first five only. Tables are provided with the Wechsler battery of tests to enable the 'raw' score on each individual test to be modified so as to be comparable with the scores on each of the other tests in the battery. These so-called 'weighted scores' are added up and the IQ is read from the tables for the appropriate age group.

The Wechsler battery of tests has been described in some detail in order to indicate as far as possible the purpose of various kinds of tests. The other tests listed above differ in content rather than in principle from those of the Wechsler series. They will, therefore, be described only briefly.

2. STANFORD–BINET TEST

This was originally a French test but has been revised by the Americans Terman and Merill and further slightly modified for use in this country. There are tests for each year of life from 2 to 14 years, a test for the average adult and three tests for superior adults.

There is a test for each 6-monthly period from 2 to 4 years, in each of which there are six subtests. Each subtest is intended to correspond roughly with 1 month of the child's life between these ages. Between 5 and 14 years there are six subtests for each 12-monthly period, so that in this age group each subtest corresponds roughly with a 2-monthly period.

The subject is first given the test corresponding to 2 years below his chronological age and then those for successive years, until no further response is obtained. For each year's test completed, he is credited with the mental age of that year and with an additional mental age of 1/12 for each subtest passed between 2 and 4 years and an additional 2/12 for each subtest between 5 and 14 years, where he has failed to pass the complete test for those years. The total so obtained is regarded as the subject's 'mental age' (MA). Additional credits are given to subjects passing all or part of the various adult tests.

Tables are provided with the Stanford–Binet test to convert the mental age to the intelligence quotient.

The Stanford–Binet test, even in its revised form, is said to penalize the mentally handicapped in the subcultural group as it is so heavily weighted with verbal and educational items. The WAIS is considered a more appropriate test for application to this group.

3. RAVEN'S MATRICES

This is a perceptual test of intelligence and is claimed to give a good assessment of general native intellectual ability without invoking social training, educational status or muscular co-ordination and speed. The subject is required to select the correct pattern, from a number of alternatives, to complete a design.

4. PORTEUS MAZE

This consists of a series of mazes of increasing complexity, there being one maze for each year of life from 3 to 14 years with the exception of year 13, for which there is no maze. There are two mazes for adults. The subject is credited with the mental age corresponding to the most difficult maze traced. Additional credit is given for completing the adult mazes. The mental ages so obtained on this test, however, are only approximate and too much reliance should not be placed on them.

5. KENT ORAL TEST

This is a quick test, which is useful for revealing obvious mental handicap, and consists of a series of fairly simple questions, but of increasing difficulty, ranging from 'What are houses made of?' to 'If your shadow points to the north-east where is the sun?'

6. MERRILL–PALMER TEST

This test is part verbal and part performance. It is, however, liable to give false results owing to social training influences, but it is useful for testing children who are thought to be mentally handicapped.

7. DREVER–COLLINS TEST

This is a performance test specially adapted for testing deaf persons who cannot comprehend spoken instructions.

TESTS SUGGESTED FOR USE WITH PRESUMED MENTALLY HANDICAPPED PERSONS

Approximate chronological age years	*Test*
0–3	None worth doing
3–7	Merrill–Palmer
7–17	Stanford–Binet
8–17	Matrices 1947 (for children 5–9 years of age normally, but can be used as check in this group). Matrices 1938 (mentally handicapped persons over 12 years)
5–15	WISC
15–60	WAIS
14 upwards	Matrices 1938
	Various performance tests

There is also a Wechsler Test specially adapted for use with blind persons.

At any age from 5 years upwards, assistance may be gained from the child's school reports.

DEVELOPMENTAL SCALES

1. GESELL DEVELOPMENTAL SCHEDULES

There is one schedule for infants up to the age of 36 months and one for the preschool child from the age of 15 months up to 6 years. These schedules provide standards of normal development of motor activity, language, adaptive behaviour and social behaviour at various ages within the above limits. They provide useful indications of progress when formal intelligence tests cannot be applied.

2. GRIFFITHS DEVELOPMENTAL SCHEDULES

The tests in these schedules were modified from those of Gesell to provide a general intelligence quotient (GQ), based on the average of quotients obtained in each of five fields of development: locomotion, personal social, speech, hand and eye, and performance (which includes the ability to reason and to manipulate material intelligently).

3. VINELAND SOCIAL MATURITY SCALE

The importance of a mentally handicapped person's social sense has been stressed above and the Vineland Social Maturity Scale is an attempt to assess this objectively from a consideration of his behaviour. The scale covers the period from birth to about 25 years, but is more useful at younger ages.

Although too much reliance cannot be placed on the results obtained from this test, they serve as useful indications of progress made as a result of training in hospital.

Each item on this scale is conceived as representing a definite step in the development of the sense of social responsibility and is expressed in some detailed performance. Consequently, the value of the detailed items is determined principally by the extent to which they reflect the growth of personal independence.

4. GUNZBURG PROGRESS ASSESSMENT CHARTS OF SOCIAL DEVELOPMENT

These charts record development under four headings: self-help, communication, socialization and occupation. A number of skills are included under each of these headings, and the charts are designed to enable easy visual comparison of those skills present on initial recording with those present on subsequent occasions, and to identify specific weaknesses.

Separate charts are used for different age groups and levels of functioning: the Primary Progress Assessment Chart (PPAC) for very young normal children and for the profoundly mentally handicapped child and adult, the Progress Assessment Chart 1 (PAC 1) for the age group 6–16 years (there is a modified form (M/PAC 1) in which the special learning difficulties of the child with Down's syndrome are taken into consideration) and the Progress Assessment Chart 2

(PAC 2), for use with teenagers and older mentally handicapped people.

A Progress Evaluation Index has been developed for use with each Progress Assessment chart, to enable the achievements of an individual on that chart to be compared with the average attainments of other mentally handicapped people of comparable intelligence.

PORTAGE

Portage is a system of recording a child's present performance in many areas and of setting goals to be achieved. It was developed for use in normal children in rural America but has been adopted by workers in mental handicap. Frequently, Portage is carried out by psychologists or, following training, it may be done by community nurses, teachers or social workers. In every case the parents are also involved. The Portage kit consists of checklists and cards and careful keeping of records is essential. During its use, goals which are set are broken down into smaller stages. In this way parents and workers regularly monitor progress in a methodical and rewarding way and it has proved to be a most effective method of teaching new skills.

PERSONALITY TESTS

As has been pointed out, some intelligence tests, as well as revealing intellectual ability, give interesting indications as to the subject's personality. To explore this field further, however, special personality or projection tests have been devised. In the Rorschach Blot Test, the subject is shown a series of ink-blots and is asked what each suggests to him. In the Szondi Test, he is asked to choose from a number of photographs of human faces those which, in his opinion, fulfil criteria suggested by the examiner, and in the Repertory Grid Test to rate each of eight pictures for various undesirable characteristics. The Eysenck–Withers Test is a test of extroversion, introversion and neuroticism, and is dependent on the subject's ability to read the instructions and, therefore, has limited use in the mentally handicapped.

Such tests are undoubtedly useful, but it is claimed by some critics that the interpretation of results is often too dependent on the examiner's own personality.

A useful projection test for the mentally handicapped is based on the Lowenfeld World Technique. The patient is provided with a sand-tray and toy equipment: fences, trees, buildings, transport, animals, people, etc. and is asked to make whatever he likes with these materials. Personality traits and disturbances are revealed in the form of the world the patient builds.

Legal Aspects of the Care of the Mentally Handicapped

THE MENTAL HEALTH ACT 1983

The Mental Health Act 1983, which received Royal Assent on 9 May 1983, consolidates the law relating to mentally disordered persons in the Mental Health Act 1959 and the Mental Health (Amendment) Act 1982.

With the exception of one or two of its provisions, the Act will come into force on 30 September 1983 and will apply only to England and Wales.

PART I

APPLICATION OF ACT

Definition of Mental Disorder

Section 1.

(2) *Mental Disorder* means mental illness, arrested or incomplete development of mind, psychopathic disorder and any other disorder or disability of mind. The subsection defines the following types of mental disorder:

Severe mental impairment—a state of arrested or incomplete development of mind, which includes *severe* impairment of intelligence and social functioning and is associated with abnormally aggressive or seriously irresponsible conduct on the part of the person concerned.

Mental impairment—a state of arrested or incomplete development of mind (not amounting to severe mental impairment), which includes *significant* impairment of intelligence and social functioning and is associated with abnormally aggressive or seriously irresponsible conduct on the part of the person concerned.

Psychopathic disorder—a persistent disorder or disability of mind (whether or not including significant impairment of intelligence), which results in abnormally aggressive or seriously irresponsible conduct on the part of the person concerned.

(3) No person is to be treated as suffering from mental disorder *by reason only* of promiscuity or other immoral conduct, sexual deviancy or dependence on alcohol or drugs.

PART II

COMPULSORY ADMISSION TO HOSPITAL AND GUARDIANSHIP

Admission for Assessment

Section 2.

This section *authorizes the detention in hospital for assessment* (or for assessment followed by medical treatment), *for a period not exceeding twenty eight days,* of any patient suffering from mental disorder, *provided* it can be shown that his mental disorder warrants this for at least a limited period, and that it is in the interests of his own health or safety or of the protection of others. An *application for admission for assessment* may be made to the managers of the hospital, either *by the nearest relative* as defined in Section 26 or *by an approved social worker,* who must have personally seen the patient within a period of fourteen days ending with the date of the application.

Where the application is made by an approved social worker, he is required before, or within a reasonable time, to take such steps as are practicable to inform the person (if any) who appears to be the patient's nearest relative of the application and of the nearest relative's power to discharge the patient under section 23 (section 11).

The application has to be founded on the *written recommendations* in the prescribed form, signed on or before the date of the application, *of two medical practitioners* who have personally examined the patient, either together or at an interval of not more than five days. One of these medical recommendations must be given by a medical practitioner approved for the purpose by the Secretary of State as having special experience in the diagnosis or treatment of mental disorder. Unless that practitioner has himself previous acquaintance with the patient, the other recommendations must, if practicable, be given by a medical practitioner with such acquaintance. Except when the application is for admission to a mental nursing home or to private beds in hospitals, *one* of the medical recommendations may be given by a practitioner on the staff of the hospital to which the patient is to be admitted. However, *both* medical recommendations may be given by practitioners on the staff of that hospital where compliance with this exclusion would result in delay involving serious risk to the health or safety of the patient or where one of the practitioners works at the hospital for less than half his contracted time with the health service or, where one of the practitioners is a consultant, the other does not work in a grade in which he is under that consultant's direction, whether at that hospital or elsewhere. In addition to these limitations, a medical recommendation may not be given by any of the following persons:

a. The applicant
b. A partner of the applicant or of a practitioner by whom another medical recommendation is given for the purposes of the same application
c. A person employed as an assistant by the applicant or by any other such practitioner as aforesaid
d. A person who receives or has an interest in the receipt of any payments made on account of the maintenance of the patient, or by the husband, wife, father, father-in-law, mother, mother-in-law, son, son-in-law, daughter, daughter-in-law, brother, brother-in-law, sister, sister-in-law of the patient or of any such person as aforesaid, or of a practitioner by whom another medical recommendation is given for purposes of the same application.

For the purposes of this section a general practitioner who is employed part time in hospital shall not be regarded as a practitioner on its staff (section 12).

The patient has the right to apply to a *Mental Health Review Tribunal* within fourteen days of admission (section 66).

Admission for Treatment

Section 3.

This section *authorizes the detention in hospital for treatment* (in the first instance *for a period not exceeding six months*—section 20) of a patient suffering from mental illness, severe mental impairment, psychopathic disorder or mental impairment, *provided* that it can be shown that his mental state makes it appropriate for him to receive medical treatment in hospital, that it is necessary for the health or safety of the patient or for the protection of other persons that he should receive such treatment and that it cannot be provided unless he is detained under this section. In the case of *psychopathic disorder or mental impairment,* it has to be shown that such treatment is likely to alleviate or prevent a deterioration of the patient's condition.

An *application for admission for treatment* under section 3 may be made either *by the nearest relative* of the patient or *by an approved social worker* after consultation with the nearest relative (and *not against his expressed objection*), unless consultation is not reasonably practicable or would involve unreasonable delay. The applicant must have seen the patient personally within a period of fourteen days ending with the date of the application (section 11).

In addition to the general requirements and limitations as to *medical recommendations* under the application for admission for assessment procedure, described above, the following requirements apply specifically in the case of the application for admission for treatment procedure under section 3:

The recommendations must state whether other methods of dealing with the patient are available and, if so, why they are not appropriate. Both recommendations must describe the patient as suffering from the *same one form* of mental disorder, although either or both may describe him as suffering from other forms in addition.

The patient must be admitted to hospital within a period of fourteen days, beginning with the date on which he was last examined by a practitioner before giving his medical recommendation (section 6). The patient may apply to a *Mental Health Review Tribunal* within a period of six months beginning with the day of his admission (section 66).

Admission for Assessment in Cases of Emergency

Section 4.

This section authorizes an *approved social worker* or *any relative of the patient*, in any case of urgent necessity, to apply for the patient's detention in hospital for assessment under section 2 if full compliance with the provisions of that section would involve unreasonable delay. The applicant must have seen the patient personally within the previous twenty-four hours.

The application may be founded on *one* medical recommendation only, given, if practicable, by a practitioner with previous acquaintance with the patient and signed on or before the date of the application. The patient must be admitted to hospital within a period of twenty-four hours beginning with the date on which he was examined by the medical practitioner giving the medical recommendation or with the date of the application, whichever is earlier (section 6).

Under this emergency procedure *a patient may be detained for seventy-two hours only*, unless a second medical recommendation (subject to the limitations defined in section 12 as regards the practitioner's relationship with the applicant or the practitioner giving the other recommendation) is given and received by the managers within that period.

Application in Respect of Patients Already in Hospital

Section 5.

This section *authorizes the detention in hospital* of any in patient, including a patient admitted for assessment, *for a period of seventy-two hours* from the time the medical practitioner in charge of the treatment of the patient furnishes the managers of the hospital with a written report that it appears to him that an application should be made for the patient's admission to hospital under one of the compulsory procedures in earlier sections. The medical practitioner may nominate one other (*and only one*) medical practitioner on the staff of the hospital to act for him in his absence.

An informal patient may also be detained in hospital for a period of up to six hours from the time a nurse, of a class prescribed by the Secretary of State, records in writing that it appears to the nurse that the patient is suffering from mental disorder to such a degree that it is necessary for his health or safety or for the protection of others for him to be immediately restrained from leaving the hospital and that it is not practicable to secure the immediate attendance of a practitioner for the purpose of furnishing the required medical report. The nurse's report must be delivered to the mangers of the hospital as soon as possible after it is made.

GUARDIANSHIP

Section 7.

This section *authorizes the reception into the guardianship* of either a social services authority or of any other person (including the applicant himself) approved by the social services authority, of any person who has attained the age of 16 years suffering from mental illness, severe mental impairment, psychopathic disorder, or mental impairment, which warrants his reception into guardianship, *provided* that it is in the interests of the welfare of the patient or for the protection of other persons. The same general provisions as to the applications and medical recommendations apply as in the case of applications for admission to hospital under section 3. However, in the case of guardianship, the application is made to the social services authority named as guardian or to the social services authority for the area in which the person named resides, with a statement that he is willing to act as guardian.

Section 8.

The *application* has to be forwarded to the local social services authority within a period of fourteen days beginning with the date on which the patient was last examined by a medical practitioner before giving a medical recommendation.

If accepted by the local social services authority, the application immediately confers on the authority or person named as guardian the power to require the patient to reside in a specified place, to attend at specified places and times for the purpose of medical treatment, occupation, education and training, and power to require access to be given at any place where the patient is residing to any registered medical practitioner, approved social worker or other specified person.

Section 9.

This section *confers on the Secretary of State the power to make regulations* requiring patients under guardianship to be visited on behalf of local social services authorities, and where some person other than the

112

local social services authority is the guardian, for the appointment of a medical practitioner to act as the nominated medical attendant.

The patient may apply to a *Mental Health Review Tribunal* within a period of six months beginning with the day on which the application is accepted (section 66).

Section 10.

If a guardian dies, or is unwilling to continue as guardian, the guardianship of the patient thereupon rests in the local authority pending the appointment of another guardian. The functions of a guardian temporarily incapacitated by illness or any other cause may be transferred during his incapacity to the local social services authority or any other person approved by that authority.

A County Court, on application by an approved social worker, may order that the guardianship of a patient be transferred to a local social services authority or to any other person approved by that authority, *if* it appears that the current guardian has performed his functions negligently or in a manner contrary to the interests of the patient.

Duties of Approved Social Workers to make Applications

Section 13.

This section *imposes a duty on an approved social worker to make an application for admission to hospital or to guardianship* of any patient within his area, where he is satisfied that such an application should be made and, having regard to any other relevant circumstances, that it is necessary or proper for the application to be made. Before making a decision, the approved social worker, is required to interview the patient. *A duty is imposed on the local social services authority to direct an approved social worker,* at the request of the nearest relative, to take the patient's case into consideration with a view to making an application for his admission to hospital and, where the approved social worker decides not to make the application, he is required to inform the nearest relative of his reasons in writing.

Section 14.

This section *imposes a duty on the managers of the hospital,* where a patient is admitted to hospital in pursuance of an application (other than an emergency application) by his nearest relative, *to notify, as soon as practicable, the local social services authority* for the area in which the patient resided immediately before his admission, and that authority is required as soon as practicable to arrange for a social worker of its department to interview the patient and provide the managers with a report on his social circumstances.

Reclassification of Patients
Section 16.

Where it appears to the appropriate medical officer that a patient detained in hospital or subject to guardianship is suffering from *a form of mental disorder other than the form or forms specified in the application,* he may furnish to the managers of the hospital or to the guardian, as the case may be, a report to that effect. The application shall then have effect as if that other form of mental disorder were specified in it. However, if the report is to the effect that a patient detained in hospital is suffering from psychopathic disorder or mental impairment, the appropriate medical officer is required to state his opinion as to whether further medical treatment in hospital is likely to alleviate or prevent a deterioration in the patient's condition. If, in his opinion, this is not likely, the managers' authority to detain the patient ceases. The managers of the hospital are required to cause the patient and his nearest relative to be informed where a report is furnished under this section.

LEAVE OF ABSENCE FROM HOSPITAL
Section 17.

The section *authorizes the responsible medical officer to grant, for any period, leave of absence* to a patient liable to be detained in hospital, subject to any conditions he considers necessary in the interests of the patient or for the protection of other persons, including the requirement that the patient shall remain during his absence in the custody of any person authorized in writing by the managers of the hospital.

A patient may not be recalled to hospital from leave of absence after he has ceased to be liable to be detained in hospital or *after the expiration of the period of six months* beginning with the first of his absence on leave, *provided* he has not returned to hospital, or been transferred to another hospital under the provisions of the Mental Health Act during this period *and provided* he is not absent without leave at the expiration of this period.

ABSENCE WITHOUT LEAVE
Section 18.

This section *authorizes the taking into custody and the return to hospital* by any approved social worker or any officer on the staff of the hospital, any constable, or any person authorized in writing by the managers of the hospital, of any patient absent without leave from the hospital or failing to return to the hospital at the expiration of a period of authorized leave or if recalled from leave, or absenting himself without permission from any place where he is required to reside as a condition of leave.

114

Similarly, this section *authorizes the taking into custody and return to his required place of residence* by any officer on the staff of a local health authority, by any constable, or by any person authorized in writing by the guardian or a local social services authority, of any patient subject to guardianship who absents himself without the leave of his guardian from his required place of residence.

A patient may *not* be taken into custody *after the period of twenty eight days beginning with the first day of his absence without leave,* nor after the expiry of the period for which he was liable to be detained under sections 2, 4, 5. After the expiry of any of the above periods the patient ceases to be liable to be detained or subject to guardianship under section 7 subject to the provisions of section 21.

TRANSFER OF PATIENTS
Section 19.

This section *authorizes the continued detention of patients liable to detention when they are transferred from one hospital to another, the transfer to the guardianship of another local social services authority* (or of any person appointed by such an authority) *of any person subject to guardianship, or the transfer into guardianship of a patient liable to detention in hospital, or vice versa.* A patient transferred from guardianship to hospital in this way, may apply to a *Mental Health Review Tribunal* within the period of six months beginning with the day on which he is transferred (section 66).

DURATION OF AUTHORITY FOR DETENTION OR GUARDIANSHIP AND DISCHARGE OF PATIENTS
Section 20.

This section *limits the authority for detention in hospital or under guardianship to a period not exceeding six months,* beginning with the day the patient was admitted to hospital or the guardianship application accepted. However, it *authorizes the detention for a further period of six months* and, *subsequently, for periods of one year at a time if,* within a period of two months ending with the last day of these periods, the responsible medical officer reports to the managers of the hospital in the prescribed form that medical treatment in hospital likely to alleviate or prevent deterioration in the condition of a patient suffering from mental illness, severe mental impairment, psychopathic disorder or mental impairment, and necessary for the health or safety of the patient or for the protection of other persons, cannot be provided unless the patient continues to be detained. However, in the case of mental illness or severe mental impairment, the unlikelihood of the patient being able to care for himself, to obtain the care which he needs, or to guard himself against serious exploitation is, for the purposes of this section, an acceptable alternative to the likelihood of medical treatment in hospital alleviating or preventing a deterioration of his condition. Before furnishing his report, the responsible medical officer is required to consult one or more other persons who have been professionally concerned with the patient's medical treatment.

The section *authorizes guardianship for further similar periods if,* within the specified period, the nominated medical attendant of a patient under guardianship reports to the guardian and social services authority in the prescribed form that it appears to him that the patient is suffering from mental illness, severe mental impairment, psychopathic disorder or mental impairment of a nature or degree which warrants his reception into guardianship and that it is necessary in the interests of the welfare of the patient or for the protection of other persons that the patient should remain under guardianship.

The managers or local social services authority are required to notify patients of each renewal of authority, and the patient may apply to a *Mental Health Review Tribunal* within the period for which the authority is renewed (section 66).

Section 21.

A patient who is *absent without leave* on the day he would otherwise cease to be liable to be detained in hospital or subject to guardianship, or within the period of one week ending with that day, remains so liable or subject *for a period of 28 days* from the day on which he is returned or returns himself to hospital or place where he ought to be, whichever is the earlier. If the patient is returned or returns himself within the 28 day period, he remains liable to be detained or subject to guardianship *for a week* from the day on which he is so returned or returns.

Section 22.

A *patient liable to be detained by virtue of an application for admission for treatment or subject to guardianship by virtue of a guardianship application,* who is *detained in custody* as the result of any sentence or court order made in the United Kingdom (including a remand order) *for a period exceeding six months,* or for successive periods exceeding in aggregate six months, *ceases to be so liable* or subject at the expiration of that period.

DISCHARGE OF PATIENTS

Section 23.

This section *authorizes the following persons to make an order in writing discharging a patient from detention or guardianship:*

The *responsible medical officer,* the *managers of the hospital* or the *nearest relative* in the case of a patient detailed in hospital for *assessment* or *treatment.*

The *responsible medical officer,* the *responsible social services authority* or the *nearest relative* in the case of a patient subject to guardianship.

The *Secretary of State in the case of a patient detained in a mental nursing home for assessment* or *treatment.*

The *Regional Health Authority, District Health Authority* or *special health authority* if the patient is maintained in a *mental nursing home under a contract with that authority.*

The powers of the authorities may be exercised by *any three or more members* of the authorities or body authorized by them on their behalf or by three or more members of a committee or subcommittee of that authority or body which has been authorized by them in that behalf.

RESTRICTIONS ON DISCHARGE BY THE NEAREST RELATIVE
Section 25.

This section *requires the nearest relative to give not less than seventy-two hours notice in writing* to the managers of the hospital of an order to discharge a patient liable to detention in hospital and *authorizes the continued detention of the patient, against the nearest relative's wishes,* if the responsible medical officer reports to the managers, *within the period of notice,* that in his opinion the patient would be *likely to act in a manner dangerous to others* or *himself if discharged.* It also denies the relative the right to order discharge again *during a period of six months* beginning with the date of the responsible medical officer's report, but requires the relative to be informed of the report and confers on him the right to apply to a *Mental Health Review Tribunal* within a period of twenty-eight days beginning with the day on which he was informed.

DEFINITION OF NEAREST RELATIVE
Section 26.

This section *lists relatives in the following order of precedence:*

  a. husband or wife
  b. son or daughter
  c. father or mother
  d. brother or sister
  e. grandparent
  f. grandchild
  g. uncle or aunt
  h. nephew or niece

117

For the purposes of the Act, *adoptive* parents are treated as though they were the *natural* parents of the patient, and *relations of the half-blood* as though they were *relatives of the whole-blood.* In each case, relatives of the whole-blood take precedence over relatives of the same description of the half-blood and the elder or eldest of two or more relatives takes precedence over the other or others of the same description, *regardless of sex.* An illegitimate child is treated as the legitimate child of his mother. However, precedence is given to relatives with whom the patient ordinarily resides or is cared for or ordinarily resided or was cared for before admission to hospital. For the purpose of this section, 'husband' and 'wife' include a person who is living with the patient as the patient's husband or wife, as the case may be or (if the patient is an in-patient), was so living until the patient was admitted, *for a period of not less than six months, provided,* in the case of a married patient, that the patient is permanently separated from the spouse by agreement or court order, or has deserted or been deserted by the spouse. A patient, other than a relative with whom the patient has ordinarily resided *for a period of not less than five years,* is treated as though he were mentioned last in the above list of precedence, with the exception that he shall *not* be treated as the nearest relative of a married patient unless the patient is permanently separated from his other spouse or has deserted or been deserted by the spouse.

Relatives are excluded from the order of precedence if

a. they are not resident in the United Kingdom, the Channel Islands and the Isle of Man if the patient is ordinarily resident there, or
b. if they are the husband or wife of the patient from whom they are permanently separated, either by agreement or court order, or have currently deserted the patient or been deserted by him, or
c. not being the husband, wife, father or mother of the patient, are under 18 years of age, or
d. a person currently subject to an order under Section 38 of the Sexual Offences Act 1956 (which relates to incest with a person under 18).

Section 27.

Where *parental rights have been assumed by a local authority or other person by virtue of the Child Care Act 1980,* that authority or person is deemed to be the nearest relative in preference to any other person except the patient's husband or wife (if any) and any parent other than the parent on whose account parental rights were assumed under Section 3 (1) of the Child Care Act 1980.

Section 28.

Where *a patient under 18 years of age* is *under the guardianship of a person not being his nearest relative* or, in the case of joint guardianship of two persons, where one is not his nearest relative, or is in the custody of a person other than his parents by virtue of matrimonial proceedings or by virtue of a separation agreement between them, that person is deemed to be his nearest relative, unless excluded from the order of the precedence by one of the provisions listed above in section 26.

TRANSFER OF NEAREST RELATIVES RIGHTS

Section 29.

This section *authorizes a County Court, upon application, to order that the functions of the nearest relative be transferred,* under circumstances defined in the section, *to any other person specified in the application, who, in the opinion of the Court, is a proper person to act as the patient's nearest relative.*

Such an *application* may be made *by any relative* of the patient, *by any other person with whom the patient is residing* or was last residing before admission to hospital, or *by an approved social worker. The nearest relative* of a patient liable to detention or subject to guardianship has *the right to apply to a Mental Health Review Tribunal* within the period of twelve months beginning with the date of the order under this section and in any subsequent period of twelve months (section 66).

Section 30.

This section *defines the persons on whose application the Court may discharge or vary its order under section 29* and the circumstances under which that order ceases to have effect.

PART III

PATIENTS CONCERNED IN CRIMINAL PROCEEDINGS OR UNDER SENTENCE

Remand to Hospital for Report on Accused's Mental Condition

Section 35.

Where a *Crown Court or Magistrates' Court* is satisfied on the written or oral evidence of a medical practitioner approved by the Secretary of State that there is reason to suspect an accused person (as defined in this section) is suffering from mental illness, psychopathic disorder, mental impairment or severe mental impairment, the Court *may remand the accused to a hospital specified by the Court for a report on his mental condition. The Court must be satisfied* also that a report on his mental condition would be impracticable if he were remanded on bail and satisfied on the written or oral evidence of the medical practitioner who would be responsible for making the report, or of some other person

119

representing the managers of the hospital, *that arrangements have been made for the accused person's admission to hospital within seven days beginning with the date of his remand.* If the Court is so satisfied it may direct his detention in a place of safety pending his hospital admission.

The *Court may further remand the accused person for up to twenty-eight days at a time, subject to an overall total of twelve weeks, if it appears to the Court on the written or oral evidence of the medical practitioner responsible for making the report that a further remand is necessary for completing the assessment of the accused's mental condition. The Court may exercise this power without* bringing the accused before the Court if he is represented by counsel or a solicitor and either is given the opportunity of being heard. *The accused person is entitled to obtain* at his own expense *an independent report on his mental condition from a medical practitioner* chosen by him and to apply to the Court on its basis for his remand to be terminated.

A Crown Court may not exercise its powers under this section in respect of a person convicted before the Court of an offence for which the sentence is fixed by law.

An accused person who absconds while in or being taken to or from the hospital to which he has been remanded *may be arrested without warrant by any constable* and shall be brought before the Court that remanded him as soon as practicable, when the Court may terminate the remand and deal with him in any way it could have done if he had not been remanded under this section.

Remand of Accused Person to Hospital for Treatment.

Section 36.

Where a *Crown Court* is satisfied on the written or oral evidence of *two* medical practitioners, of whom *at least one* must be approved by the Secretary of State, that an accused person (as defined in this section) is suffering from mental illness, or severe mental impairment of a nature or degree which makes it appropriate for him to be detained in hospital for medical treatment, it *may remand him to a hospital specified by the Court instead of remanding him in custody.* The *Court must be satisfied* also on the written or oral evidence of the medical practitioner, who would be in charge of the accused's treatment, or of some other person representing the managers of the hospital, *that arrangements have been made for his admission to hospital within the period of seven days beginning with the date of the remand.* If the Court is so satisfied, it may direct his detention in a place of safety pending his hospital admission.

The Court *may further remand the accused person for up to twenty-eight days at a time, subject to an overall limit of twelve weeks,* if it appears to the Court on the written or oral evidence of the responsible medical officer that a further remand is warranted. The Court may exercise his power *without* bringing the accused before the Court if he is represented by counsel or a solicitor and either is given the opportunity of being heard.

The *accused person is entitled to obtain,* at his own expense, *an independent report on his mental condition from a medical practitioner* chosen by him and to apply to the Court on its basis for his remand to be terminated.

A Crown Court may not exercise its powers under this section in respect of a person awaiting trial before the Court for an offence for which the sentence is fixed by law.

An accused person who absconds while in or being taken to or from a hospital to which he has been remanded, *may be arrested without warrant by any constable* and shall be brought before the Court that remanded him as soon as practicable, when the Court may terminate the remand and deal with him in any way it could have done if he had not been remanded under this section.

Powers of Courts to Order Hospital Admission or Guardianship

Section 37.

This section *authorizes a Crown Court* (in the case of a patient convicted before it of an offence punishable with imprisonment), *or a Magistrates' Court* (in the case of a person convicted of an offence punishable on summary conviction), *to order that person's admission to, and detention in a specified hospital—'hospital order'—*or to *place him under the guardianship of a local social services authority* or any other specified person approved by a local social services department—*'guardianship order'.* Before making this order the Court must be satisfied on the written or oral evidence of *two* medical practitioners, *at least one* of whom must be approved by the Secretary of State, that the offender is suffering from mental illness, psychopathic disorder, mental impairment or severe mental impairment which makes it appropriate for him to be detained in hospital for medical treatment, and, in the case of psychopathic disorder or mental impairment, that such treatment is likely to alleviate or prevent a deterioration of his condition. The Court *must also be satisfied* on the written or oral evidence of the medical practitioner, who would be in charge of the offender's treatment or of some other person representing the managers of the hospital, *that arrangements have been made for his admission to the hospital in question within twenty-eight days beginning with the date of the order. Before making a guardianship order, the Court must be satisfied that the offender has attained the age of 16 years and that his mental disorder warrants his reception into guardianship and that the local* *social services authority is willing to receive him into guardianship.* A Magistrates' Court may make an order under this section *without* convicting a person suffering from mental illness or severe mental impairment, *provided* the Court is satisfied he did the act.

Interim Hospital Orders

Section 38.

Where a Crown Court is satisfied on the written or oral evidence *of two* medical practitioners, of whom *at least one* must be approved by the Secretary of State, *that an offender convicted before it of an offence punishable with imprisonment* (other than an offence the sentence for which is fixed by law) *is suffering from mental illness, psychopathic disorder, mental impairment or severe mental impairment,* and the Court has reason to suppose that it may be appropriate for a hospital order to be made, *it may make an interim hospital order authorizing his admission to a specified hospital and his detention there for up to twelve weeks. At least one* of the two medical practitioners must be employed at the hospital. *The Court must be satisfied* also on the written or oral evidence of the medical practitioner, who would be in charge of his treatment or some other person representing the managers of the hospital, that arrangements have been made for his admission to hospital within the period of twenty-eight days beginning with the date of the order. If the Court is so satisfied, it may direct his detention in a place of safety pending his hospital admission.

The *Court may renew the interim hospital order for up to twenty-eight days, subject to an overall limit of six months, if it appears to the Court on the written or oral evidence of the responsible medical officer that continuation of the order is warranted. The Court may exercise this power without* bringing the offender before the Court if he is represented by counsel or a solicitor and either is given the opportunity of being heard. *A Magistrates' Court,* which is similarly satisfied in *the case of a person convicted before it of an offence punishable on summary conviction with imprisonment, may also make and renew an interim hospital order as above.*

An offender subject to an interim hospital order, who absconds while in or being taken to or from hospital, *may be arrested without warrant by any constable* and shall be brought before the Court that made the order, as soon as practicable, when the Court may terminate the order and deal with him in any way it could have done if it had not made the order.

Both the Crown Court and Magistrates' Court may make a hospital order on an offender subject to an interim hospital order without bringing him before the Court if he is represented by counsel or a solicitor and either is given the opportunity of being heard.

An interim hospital order terminates when the Court makes a hospital order, decides after considering the written or oral evidence of the responsible medical officer *to deal with the offender in some other way, or at the end of six months from the date when it was first made.*

Mental Condition of Persons Accused of Murder

The Bail Act 1976 was amended by the Mental Health (Amendment) Act 1982 so as *to require a Court granting bail to a person accused of murder to impose as a condition of bail that the accused shall undergo an examination of his mental condition by two medical practitioners, at least one* of whom must be approved under section 12, unless the Court is satisfied that satisfactory reports on his mental condition have already been obtained.

Information as to Hospitals

Section 39.

This section *imposes a duty on Regional Health Authorities to supply the Court with information on request as to what arrangements could be made for the admission of persons for whom the Court is contemplating making a hospital order or interim hospital order.*

Restriction Orders

Section 41.

This section *authorizes a Crown Court to impose an order restricting the patient's discharge ('restriction order') and any of the following special restrictions,* either indefinitely or for a specified period, *where this is considered necessary for the protection of the public,* provided that the medical evidence of *at least one of* the medical practitioners was given orally in Court:

During the period that discharge is restricted, the normal limit to the duration of the authority for detention does *not* apply. The *consent of the Secretary of State is necessary* before the patient can be transferred to another hospital or to guardianship or vice versa or before he can be granted leave, and he can be recalled from leave at any time while the order restricting discharge is in force. The *Secretary of State's consent* is also necessary before the patient may be discharged by any of the persons who normally have this power. The *responsible medical officer* is required to examine a person subject to a restriction order at such intervals of a year or less as the Secretary of State may direct, and to report to him on that person.

A *patient subject to a restriction order ('restricted patient')* may apply to a *Mental Health Review Tribunal* within a period between the expiration of six months and the expiration of twelve months beginning with the date of the relevant hospital order of transfer direction, and in any subsequent period of twelve months (section 70).

The *Secretary of State may* at any time refer the case of a restricted patient to a *Mental Health Review Tribunal,* and *is required* to do so if the patient's case has not been considered within the last three years (section 71).

The *Mental Health Review Tribunal* is required to discharge a restricted patient absolutely if it is satisfied that it is not necessary in the interests of his health or safety or for the protection of others for him to be detained and that it is not appropriate for the patient to remain liable to be recalled to hospital for further treatment. Where the Tribunal is not satisfied that the latter condition is satisfied, it is required to direct the conditional discharge of any patient, who remains subject to recall to hospital by the Secretary of State and subject to any conditions imposed by him at the time or subsequently. The Tribunal may defer a direction for the conditional discharge of a patient until such arrangements as appear necessary to the Tribunal have been made (section 73).

Where a restricted patient who has been conditionally discharged is subsequently recalled to hospital, the *Secretary of State is required to refer his case to a Mental Health Review Tribunal* within one month of the day of the patient's return to hospital, and the patient has the right to apply to the Tribunal under section 70 during the period specified in that section, beginning with the day of the patient's return. Where a restricted patient who has been conditionally discharged has not been recalled to hospital, he may apply to a *Mental Health Review Tribunal* in the period between the expiration of twelve months and two years, beginning with the date on which he was conditionally discharged, and in any subsequent period of two years. On each of these occasions the Tribunal may vary any of the conditions to which the patient is subject or impose new conditions or may direct that the restriction order or restriction direction shall cease to have effect (section 75).

Section 42.

This section *authorizes the Secretary of State to lift the restriction order if* he is satisfied that it is no longer required for the protection of the public from serious harm. At any time while the restriction order is in force the *Secretary of State* may, if he thinks fit, by warrant discharge the patient from hospital, either absolutely or subject to conditions and in the latter case may by warrant recall a patient conditionally discharged to hospital.

Section 43.

Where a *Magistrates' Court* convicts a person aged 14 years or over of an offence punishable on summary conviction with imprisonment, and, where the conditions of section 37 above are satisfied, the court

124

may, instead of making a hospital order, remand the person in custody to be dealt with by the Crown Court, provided the Magistrates' Court is satisfied that the risk of his committing further offences is large. The Crown Court may either make a hospital order, with or without a restriction order, or may deal with the case in any other manner the Magistrates' Court might have dealt with it.

Section 44.

Pending the person's appearance before the Crown Court, the Magistrates' Court may direct his admission to the hospital, provided it is satisfied on written or oral evidence that arrangements have been made for his admission there in the event of an order being made under section 43.

Section 45.

This section *authorizes a patient,* subject to a hospital order or guardianship order made by a Magistrates' Court without convicting him, *to appeal against the order* as if it had been made on his conviction. Similarly, an appeal against such an order or against the finding upon which it was made with respect to a child or young person may be brought by him or by his parent or guardian on his behalf.

Transfer to Hospital of Prisoners, etc.

Section 47.

This section *authorizes the Secretary of State to make a 'transfer direction' (with or without a 'restriction direction')* under which a person serving a sentence of imprisonment is transferred *to a hospital (not a mental nursing home) for medical treatment, if* he is satisfied on the reports of at least two medical practitioners that the person is suffering from mental illness, psychopathic disorder, mental impairment or severe mental impairment. The Secretary of State must be satisfied that it is appropriate for the person to be detained in hospital for medical treatment and, in the case of psychopathic disorder or mental impairment, that there is a likelihood of such medical treatment alleviating or preventing a deterioration of the person's condition and, in all cases, that the transfer is in the public interest. *At least one* of the medical practitioners giving reports must be approved by the Secretary of State as having special experience in the diagnosis or treatment of mental disorders (section 54). Each must describe the patient as suffering from the *same one* form of mental disorder, although either or both may describe him as suffering from other forms as well.

A transfer direction ceases to have effect fourteen days after the date on which it is given, unless the person has been received into the hospital specified within that period.

Where no restriction direction is made, the transfer direction has the same effect as a hospital order. Where a restriction direction is made, the transfer direction has the same effect as an order under section 41. The patient has the *right of appeal to a Mental Health Tribunal* appropriate to each section (section 69).

Section 48.

This section *authorizes the Secretary of State, if* he is satisfied on similar reports to those required under section 47, that a person not serving a prison sentence is suffering from mental illness or severe mental impairment, which makes it appropriate for him to be detained in hospital for medical treatment of which he is in urgent need, *to order that person's transfer to hospital* from the various forms of custody specified in the section, including civil imprisonment and detention under the Immigration Act 1971. A transfer direction ceases to have effect fourteen days after the date on which it is given, unless the person has been received into the hospital specified within that period (section 47). Unless the Secretary of State has given a restriction direction under section 49, the transfer direction on a patient in either of the latter two categories ceases to have effect at the expiration of the period during which he would have been liable to be detained had he not been removed to hospital. If during that period the responsible medical officer, any other medical practitioner or a *Mental Health Review Tribunal* notify the Secretary of State that such a patient, subject to a transfer direction and restriction direction, no longer requires treatment in hospital for mental disorder or that no effective treatment for his disorder can be given there, the Secretary of State may direct that the patient may be removed to any place where he might have been detained, had he not been removed to hospital (section 53). A *Mental Health Review Tribunal is required to notify the Secretary of State* if in its opinion a patient subject to a restriction direction or transfer to hospital under this section would, if subject to a restriction order, be entitled to be absolutely or conditionally discharged. If the Tribunal notifies the Secretary of State that the patient would be entitled to be conditionally discharged, *it may* recommend that in the event of his not being discharged he should continue to be detained in hospital. Unless the Tribunal make such a recommendation, the Secretary of State may by warrant direct that the patient be removed to prison or other institution in which he might have been detained had he not been removed to hospital (section 74).

The *Mental Health Review Tribunal is required to notify the Secretary of State* whether, in their opinion, a restricted patient subject to a restriction direction under section 49, would if subject to a restriction order, be entitled to be absolutely or conditionally discharged under section 73 above and in the latter case may recommend that, if not discharged, the patient should continue to be detained in hospital.

If the Tribunal do not make this recommendation in the case of a patient subject to a transfer direction under section 48, the *Secretary of State* is required to direct that the patient be remitted to a prison or other institution in which he might have been detained if he had not been removed to hospital.

If, within the period of ninety days beginning with the notification by the Tribunal of its opinion that a restricted patient would be entitled to either form of discharge, the *Secretary of State* notifies the Tribunal that the patient may be so discharged, the Tribunal *shall* direct the discharge of the patient accordingly. Where the *Secretary of State* does not notify the Tribunal in this way and the Tribunal have not previously recommended that, if not discharged, the patient should remain in hospital, the managers of the hospital are required to transfer the patient to a prison or other institution where he might have been detained if he had not been removed to hospital (section 74).

Section 50.

This section *authorizes the Secretary of State to direct the transfer back to prison* of any patient subject to an order restricting his discharge, on notification by the responsible medical officer, any other medical practitioner of a *Mental Health Review Tribunal* that the patient no longer requires treatment in hospital for mental disorder or that no effective treatment for his disorder can be given in hospital, *provided* the period of his prison sentence has not expired, taking into consideration any period of remission he might have earned had he not been transferred to hospital.

Section 51.

This section *authorizes the Secretary of State to take this step under similar circumstances* in the case of patients, other than civil prisoners or those detained under the Immigration Act 1971, transferred to hospital under section 48, at any time before those cases are disposed of by the Court. In the absence of a direction from the Secretary of State, the Court itself may order the patients' return to prison or may release them on bail. This section also *authorizes a Court to make a hospital order* (with or without a restriction order) in the case of the same patients, if it appears to be impracticable or inappropriate to bring them before the Court, *provided the Court is satisfied on the written or oral evidence of at least two* medical practitioners (*one at least* approved by the Secretary of State) that the person is suffering from mental illness or severe mental impairment, which makes it appropriate for the patient to be detained in hospital for medical treatment, and that it is proper to make such an order.

127

PART IV

CONSENT TO TREATMENT

This is a completely new part of the Act introduced by the Mental Health (Amendment) Act 1982 and *concerns both detained and informal patients.*

Treatment Requiring Consent *and* a Second Opinion

Section 57.

Neither a detained nor an informal patient may be given medical treatment for mental disorder, which involves *any surgical operation for destroying brain tissue or for destroying the functioning of brain tissue* or such other forms of treatment as may be specified by regulations made by the Secretary of State, unless the patient himself has consented and a medical practitioner, other than the responsible medical officer and two other persons appointed by the Secretary of State who are not medical practitioners, have certified in writing that the patient is capable of understanding the nature, purpose and likely effects of the treatment in question and has consented to it. *The medical practitioner has to certify in writing that, having regard to the likelihood of the treatment alleviating or preventing a deterioration of the patient's condition, the treatment should be given.* Before giving this certificate, the medical practitioner must consult two other persons who have been professionally concerned with the patient's treatment, one being a nurse and the other neither a nurse nor a medical practitioner. *The responsible medical officer is required to give a report on a detained patient's condition to the Secretary of State* on the next occasion he furnishes a report under section 20 for the renewal of authority for the patient's detention and at any other time the Secretary of State may require. Where the patient is subject to a restriction direction, the responsible medical officer is required to make the report at the end of a period of six months from the date of the order, where treatment has been started within that period and, where treatment is started subsequently, on the next occasion, the responsible medical officer is otherwise required to examine and report on any restricted patient under section 41 or 49 above (section 61).

Treatment Requiring Consent *or* a Second Opinion

Section 58.

A detained patient may not be given such forms of medical treatment for mental disorder as may be specified by regulations made by the Secretary of State, unless the patient himself has consented to the treatment and either the responsible medical officer or a medical practitioner appointed by the Secretary of State has certified in writing that the patient is capable of understanding its nature, purpose and likely effects and has consented to it, or a medical practitioner similarly appointed other than the responsible medical officer, has certified in writing that the patient is not capable of understanding the nature, purpose and likely effects of that treatment or has not consented to it but that, having regard to the likelihood of its alleviating or preventing a deterioration of his condition, the treatment should be given. Before giving the certificate, the medical practitioner concerned is required to consult two other persons, who have been professionally concerned with the patient's medical treatment, one of whom must be a nurse and the other neither a nurse nor a medical practitioner. Medicine for his mental disorder may not be administered to a detained patient by any means for more than three months from when it was first administered unless the above conditions have been complied with. Where a detained patient is given treatment without his consent in accordance with this section, *the responsible medical officer is required to give a report on the patient's condition to the Secretary of State* on the next occasion he furnishes a report under section 20 for renewal of authority for the patient's detention and at any other time the Secretary of State may require. Where the patient is subject to a restriction order or restriction direction, the responsible medical officer is required to make the report at the end of a period of six months from the date of the order where treatment has been started within that period and, where treatment is started subsequently, on the next occasion the responsible medical officer is otherwise required to examine and report on any restricted patient under section 41 or 49 above (section 61).

Section 59.

Any consent or certificate under sections 57 and 58 may relate to *a plan of treatment* under which the patient is to be given one of the forms of treatment specified.

Section 60.

The *patient may withdraw his consent to treatment* at any time before its completion, but the responsible medical officer may continue the treatment if he considers discontinuation would cause serious suffering to the patient (section 62).

Section 62.

The restrictions on treatment of sections 57 and 58 do *not* apply to any treatment which is immediately necessary to save the patient's life, or which (not being irreversible) is immediately necessary to prevent a serious deterioration of his condition, or (not being irreversible or hazardous) is immediately necessary to alleviate serious suffering by the patient, or which (not being irreversible or hazardous) is immediately necessary and represents the minimum interference necessary to prevent the patient from behaving violently or being a danger to himself or others.

Treatment is defined as *irreversible* if it has unfavourable irreversible physical or psychological consequences and as *hazardous* if it entails significant physical hazard.

PART V

MENTAL HEALTH REVIEW TRIBUNALS

Constitution etc.

Section 65.

This section *requires the continuation of a Mental Health Review Tribunal* for every Regional Health Authority and for Wales under their constitution set out in Schedule 2 to the Act. The jurisdiction of a Mental Health Review may be exercised by any three or more of its members.

Applications and References Concerning Part II Patients

Section 66.

An application may be made to a Mental Health Tribunal

a. by a patient within 14 days of his admission to hospital for *assessment*

b. by a patient within six months of his admission to hospital for *treatment*

c. by a patient within six months of his *reception into guardianship*

d. by the nearest relative within twenty-eight days of his being informed that a report has been furnished under section 16 *reclassifying the patient*

e. by a patient within six months of his *transfer from guardianship to hospital* under section 19

f. by a patient within the *period of renewal* of the authority for his detention in hospital or guardianship under section 20

g. by the nearest relative within twenty-eight days of a report furnished under section 25 *restricting the nearest relative's right to discharge the patient*

h. by the nearest relative within twelve months of the *appointment by a County Court of an acting nearest relative* under section 29, and in any subsequent period of twelve months during which the order continues in force.

130

Section 67.

This section *authorizes the Secretary of State to refer the case of any patient liable to be detained or subject to guardianship, to a Mental Health Review Tribunal* at any time he thinks fit.

Duties of Managers of Hospitals to Refer Cases to Tribunals

Section 68.

The *managers of the hospital* where a patient who is detained as the result of an application for admission for treatment or on transfer from guardianship does not exercise his right to apply to a Mental Health Review Tribunal, *are required to refer the case to the Tribunal* at the expiration of the period for making such an application, unless an application or reference in respect of the patient has then been made under one of the other sections of the Act which require the Tribunal to consider his case. The managers are required to refer the case to a Tribunal, also, where authority for his detention in hospital is renewed under section 20 and three years (or one year if the patient has not attained the age of 16 years) have elapsed since his case was last considered by a Tribunal. For the purposes of this section a patient who applies to a Tribunal but subsequently withdraws his application is treated as not having exercised his right to apply.

Section 69.

This section *authorizes the nearest relative of a patient admitted to hospital in pursuance of a hospital order, to apply to a Mental Health Review Tribunal* within the period between the expiry of six months and the expiration of twelve months beginning with the date of the order and in any subsequent period of twelve months. The *nearest relative of a patient placed under guardianship order may apply* between the period of twelve months beginning with the date of the order and in any subsequent period of twelve months.

Applications to Tribunals Concerning Restricted Patients

Section 70.

This section *authorizes a patient subject to a restriction order or restricted direction to apply to a Mental Health Review Tribunal* in the period between the expiration of six months and the expiration of twelve months beginning with the date of the relevant hospital order or transfer direction and in any subsequent period of twelve months.

Section 71.

This section *authorizes the Secretary of State to refer the case of a restricted patient to a Mental Health Review Tribunal* at any time and

131

requires him to do so in the case of any restricted patient detained in hospital whose case has not been considered by such a Tribunal within the last three years.

Discharge of Patients

Powers of Tribunals

Section 72.

This section *requires the Mental Health Review Tribunal to direct the discharge of a patient liable to be detained under section 2* (for assessment) if they are satisfied that he is not suffering from mental disorder or from mental disorder of a nature or degree which warrants his detention in a hospital for assessment (or for assessment followed by medical treatment) for at least a limited period, or that his detention is not justified in the interests of his own health or safety or for the protection of others.

The section also *requires the Mental Health Review Tribunal to direct the discharge of a patient liable to be detained, other than under section 2,* if it is satisfied that he is not then suffering from mental illness, psychopathic disorder, mental impairment or severe mental impairment of a nature or degree which makes it appropriate for him to be liable to be detained in hospital for medical treatment, or that it is not necessary for his health or safety or for the protection of other persons that he should receive such treatment, or (where the nearest relative's order for the patient's discharge has been nullified, under section 25) that the patient, if released, would not be likely to act in a manner dangerous to other persons or himself.

In reaching its decision, in cases other than those detained under section 2, the Tribunal must have regard to the likelihood of medical treatment alleviating or preventing a deterioration in the patient's condition and, in the case of a patient suffering from mental illness or severe mental impairment, the likelihood of the patient being able to care for himself, to obtain the care he needs or to guard himself against serious exploitation if discharged. A Tribunal may direct the discharge of a patient on a future specified date. Where the Tribunal does not direct the discharge of a patient it may, with a view to facilitating his discharge on a future date, recommend that he be granted leave of absence or be transferred to another hospital or into guardianship and may further consider his case in the event of any of these recommendations not being complied with.

A Tribunal is similarly required to direct the discharge of a patient from guardianship if it is satisfied that he is not then suffering from mental illness, psychopathic disorder, mental impairment or severe mental impairment and that it is not necessary in the interests of the

132

welfare of the patient or for the protection of others for him to remain under guardianship.

If the Mental Health Review Tribunal does not order discharge, it may direct that the form of mental disorder specified in the relevant application, order or direction be amended to a more appropriate form if it is satisfied that the patient is suffering from this.

Sections 73–75.

These sections are dealt with following sections 41 and 49 above.

PART VI
REMOVAL AND RETURN OF PATIENTS WITHIN UNITED KINGDOM, ETC.

Section 80.

This section *permits the Secretary of State to authorize the removal of patients liable to be detained or subject to guardianship,* otherwise than by virtue of sections 35, 36 or 38, *from England or Wales to Scotland, provided* he is satisfied that it is in the interests of the patient and that the necessary arrangements have been made in Scotland. A restriction order or restriction direction of limited duration continues after transfer for the balance of its unexpired period.

Section 81.

This section *permits the Secretary of State,* under conditions similar to those in section 80, *to authorize the removal of patients liable to be detained or subject to guardianship from England or Wales to Northern Ireland.*

Section 82.

This section defines the circumstances under which the responsible authority, in the case of a patient liable to be detained or subject to guardianship under the Mental Health Act (Northern Ireland) 1961, may authorize his removal to England or Wales.

Sections 83 to 85.

The sections concern the removal of patients to and from the Channel Islands and Isle of Man.

Section 86.

This section concerns the removal of aliens.

Sections 87 to 89.

These sections concern the return of patients absent without leave from hospitals in Northern Ireland, England and Wales or the Channel Islands or Isle of Man.

PART VII

MANAGEMENT OF PROPERTY AND AFFAIRS OF PATIENTS

This is dealt with in sections 93 and 113, which are principally concerned with the appointment by the Lord Chancellor of *'nominated judges'*, the *Master of the Court of Protection* and *panels of Medical, Legal and General Lord Chancellor's Visitors,* the appointment by the Court of receivers and with the functions and powers of each of the foregoing in the management of the property and affairs of patients while they are mentally disordered.

PART VIII

MISCELLANEOUS FUNCTIONS OF LOCAL AUTHORITIES AND THE SECRETARY OF STATE

Approved Social Workers

Section 114.

This section *requires local social services authorities to appoint a sufficient number of approved social workers with appropriate competence* in dealing with persons who are suffering from mental disorder, for the purpose of discharging the functions imposed upon them by the Act.

Section 115.

This section *authorizes an approved social worker to enter and inspect any premises other than a hospital* in the area of his employing authority in which a mentally disordered person is living, if he has reasonable cause to believe that the patient is not under proper care.

Section 116.

This section *imposes a duty on local social services authorities to arrange to visit those patients in hospitals or nursing homes* in England and Wales for whom the parental rights have been vested in the local authority or who are subject to the guardianship of the authority or in whose case the functions of the nearest relative have for the time being been transferred to the local social services authority.

After Care

Section 117.

This section *imposes a duty on the District Health Authority and the local social services authority to provide,* in co-operation with relevant social agencies, *after-care services for any person who leaves hospital* where he had been detained under sections 3, 37, 47 or 48, until the authorities are satisfied that he no longer needs their services.

Code of Practice
Section 118.

The *Secretary of State is required,* after consultation with such bodies as appear to him to be concerned, *to prepare and from time to time revise a code of practice* for the guidance of medical practitioners, managers and staff of hospitals and mental nursing homes and mental welfare officers in relation to the admission of patients to hospitals and mental nursing homes under the Act, and for the guidance of medical practitioners and members of other professions in relation to the medical treatment of patients suffering from mental disorder.

The code must specify forms of medical treatment in addition to those specified under section 43 which, in the Secretary of State's opinion, give rise to special concern and should therefore not be given by a medical practitioner without the patient's consent and a certificate in writing, given in accordance with the requirements of that section by a medical practitioner approved for the purpose by the Secretary of State.

The *Secretary of State is required to lay the code and any alteration in it before Parliament* and, unless within forty days either House passes a resolution requiring the code or any alteration in it to be withdrawn, he is required to publish the code currently in force.

General Protection of Patients
Section 120.

This section *requires the Secretary of State to arrange for persons authorized by him to visit and interview in private patients detained under the Act in hospitals and mental nursing homes,* and to investigate any complaint made by a person who considers that the managers of the hospital or mental nursing home have not satisfactorily dealt with any complaint he has made while he was detained there. The Secretary of State may also require persons authorized by him to investigate any other complaint as to the exercise of the powers or the discharge of the duties concerning a person who is, or has been, detained under the Act.

A medical practitioner visiting a patient in a mental nursing home is authorized to examine him in private and to require the production for his own inspection of any records relating to the detention or treatment of any person who is, or has been, detained in a mental nursing home.

Mental Health Act Commission
Section 121.

This section *requires the Secretary of State to establish a Mental Health Act Commission* to appoint on his behalf medical practitioners

135

for the purposes of Part IV of the Act (consent to treatment) and section 118 (code of practice) and other persons for the purposes of section 57, and to perform on his behalf the functions of the Secretary of State under sections 61 and 120.

Other duties of the Commission may include, if directed by the Secretary of State, keeping under review the care and treatment or any aspect of the care and treatment of informal patients in hospitals and mental nursing homes. For this purpose, any person authorized by the Commission may visit and interview and, if he is a medical practitioner, examine in private any informal patient in a mental nursing home and may require the production for his inspection of any records relating to the treatment of any person who is, or has been, a patient in a mental nursing home.

The Commission is required to review any decision under section 134 (1) (b) to withhold from the post office a postal packet (or anything contained in it) from a patient detained in a special hospital, if the patient applies within six months of the decision. The Commission is similarly required to review a decision, under section 134 (2), to withhold from a patient detained in a special hospital a packet addressed to him if the patient or the person by whom the postal packet was sent applies within the same period. In each case the Commission may direct that the postal packet shall not be withheld.

The *Commission is required,* in the second year after its establishment and, subsequently, in every second year, *to publish a report on its activities to be laid before Parliament.*

PART IX

OFFENCES

Ill-Treatment of Patients

Section 127.

This section *renders it an offence* for any officer on the staff of a hospital or mental nursing home, for anyone otherwise employed there or for any of the managers *to ill-treat or wilfully neglect a patient receiving treatment* for mental disorder *as an in-patient,* or on the premises of the hospital or home where the patient is attending for treatment for mental disorder *as an out-patient.* It is also an offence for any individual to ill-treat or wilfully neglect a mentally disordered person while he is subject to his *guardianship* under the Act or in his custody or care.

The *penalties* for the above offences are, *on summary conviction,* a term of imprisonment not exceeding six months or a fine not exceeding the statutory maximum or both or, *on conviction on indictment,* a term of imprisonment not exceeding two years or a fine, or both.

No *proceedings may be instituted without the consent of the Director of Public Prosecutions.*

Assisting Patients to Absent Themselves without Leave

Section 128.

This section *renders it an offence to induce or knowingly assist a patient detained in hospital or subject to guardianship under this Act to absent himself without leave* or to escape from legal custody or knowingly to harbour a patient absent without leave or to assist him to prevent, hinder or interfere with his being taken into custody or returned to hospital or where he should be under guardianship.

The *penalties* for the above offences are, *on summary conviction,* a term of imprisonment not exceeding six months or a fine not exceeding the statutory maximum or both or, *on conviction on indictment,* a term of imprisonment not exceeding two years or a fine, or both.

Amendment of Sexual Offences Act 1956

The Sexual Offences Act 1956 as amended by section 127 of the Mental Health Act 1959 and the Mental Health (Amendment) Act 1982, renders it an offence for a man to have unlawful sexual intercourse with a woman suffering from *severe* mental impairment (but *not* with a woman suffering from *mental* impairment, except under section 128, Mental Health Act 1959) *provided* he knows or has reason to suspect her to be severely mentally impaired.

Sexual Intercourse with Patients

Under section 128 Mental Health Act 1959 (which was not repealed by the Mental Health (Amendment) Act 1982) it remains *an offence* for an officer on the staff of a hospital or mental nursing home, for anyone otherwise employed there or for any of the managers *to have unlawful sexual intercourse on hospital premises* with a woman receiving treatment for mental disorder there, either *as an in-patient or as an out-patient.*

It is also an offence for a man to have unlawful sexual intercourse with a mentally disordered woman subject to his *guardianship* or otherwise in his custody or care under this Act or as a resident in a residential home for mentally disordered persons. *In each case under this section it must be shown that the man knew or had reason to suspect that the woman was a mentally disordered person.*

No action may be taken under this section without the consent of the Director of Public Prosecutions.

The *penalty* for this offence *on conviction on indictment* is a term of imprisonment not exceeding two years.

137

PART X

MISCELLANEOUS AND SUPPLEMENTARY

Informal Admission of Patients

Section 131.

This section *permits* the informal admission to a hospital or mental nursing home of any patient who requires treatment for mental disorder without any powers of detention there or *permits* him to remain there, if he wishes, after he has ceased to be liable to be detained. A minor, aged 16 years or over, capable of expressing his own wishes, may make such arrangements irrespective of the wishes of his parent or guardian.

Duties of Managers of Hospitals to Give Information to Detained Patients

Section 132.

This section *requires the managers of a hospital or mental nursing home* in which a patient is detained to take such steps as are practicable and as soon as practicable after the commencement of his detention *to ensure that he understands—*

under which of the provisions of the Act he is being detained and the effect of that provision

his rights of applying to a Mental Health Review Tribunal in respect of his detention

the effects, so far as relevant to his case, of sections 23 and 25 (discharge by responsible medical officer, managers, nearest relative, etc.) and of sections 56 to 64 (Consent to Treatment), 118 (Codes of Practice), 120 (General Protection of Patients) and 134 (Correspondence of Patients).

The information must be given to the patient both orally and in writing. Unless the patient requests otherwise, the managers are required to take such steps as are practicable to furnish the person (if any) appearing to be his nearest relative with a copy of the above information given to the patient, at the same time or within a reasonable time thereafter.

Duties of Managers of Hospitals to Inform Nearest Relatives of Discharge

Section 133.

This section *requires the managers of a hospital or mental nursing home* in which a detained patient is about to be discharged *to notify the person (if any) who appears to be the nearest relative,* if practicable at least seven days before the date of discharge, except where the nearest relative is ordering discharge or where the patient or his nearest relative has requested that information about the patient's discharge should not be given.

Correspondence of Patients

Section 134.

The managers of a hospital, or a person on the staff of the hospital appointed by them for the purpose, may withhold from the post office a postal packet addressed by a patient *detained* in the hospital to any person who has requested that communications addressed to him by the patient should be withheld.

In the case of patients *detained* in a special hospital, the managers, or person on the staff of the hospital appointed by them for the purpose, may similarly withhold from the post office a postal packet addressed by the patient to any person who has requested that communications addressed to him by the patient should be withheld, or if they consider that the packet is likely to cause distress to the person to whom it is addressed or to any other person (*not being a person on the staff of the hospital*) or to cause danger to any person.

However, *no postal packet may be withheld if addressed by a patient or sent to a patient by or on behalf of the following:*

a. any Minister of the Crown or Member of either House of Parliament

b. the Master or any other officer of the Court of Protection or any of the Lord Chancellor's Visitors

c. the Parliamentary Commissioner for Administration, the Health Service Commissioner for England, the Health Service Commissioner for Wales or a Local Commissioner within the meaning of Part III of the Local Government Act 1974

d. A Mental Health Review Tribunal

e. a health authority within the meaning of the National Health Service Act 1977, a local social services authority, a Community Health Council or a probation and after-care committee appointed under paragraph 2 of Schedule 3 to the Powers of Criminal Courts Act 1973

f. the managers of the hospital in which the patient is detained

g. any legally qualified person instructed by the patient to act as his legal advisor or

h. the European Commission of Human Rights or the European Court of Human Rights

In all cases, where a postal packet is withheld from the post or from a patient, the managers are required to record the fact in writing and in the case of a patient detained in a special hospital they are required to notify the patient in writing within seven days and the person (if known) by whom the postal packet was sent.

Warrant to Search for and Remove Patients

Section 135.

This section *authorizes a Justice of the Peace to issue a warrant authorizing a constable to enter,* if need be by force, any premises within his jurisprudence specified in the warrant and, if thought fit, *to remove from there to a place of safety,* pending arrangements for his treatment or care, any person (who need *not* be named in the warrant) whom the magistrate has on information sworn by an approved social worker reasonable cause to suspect to be suffering from mental disorder and to have been or to be ill-treated, neglected or not kept under proper control or to be living alone and unable to care for himself. The constable *must* be accompanied in the execution of the warrant by an *approved social worker* and by a *medical practitioner.*

This section also *authorizes a Justice of the Peace* on the sworn evidence of any constable or any other person authorized under this Act to take a patient to any place or to take into custody or retake a patient, *to issue a warrant authorizing any named constable to enter any premises,* if need be by force, and *to remove from there any patient liable to be taken or retaken,* provided admission to the premises has been refused or if such a refusal is apprehended. The constable *may* be accompanied in the execution of the warrant by a *medical practitioner* or by *any person authorized* under the Act to take or retake the patient.

A patient removed to a *place of safety* under this section may be detained there for a period *not exceeding seventy-two hours.* A *'place of safety'* is defined as residential accommodation provided by a local social services authority under Part III of the National Health Service Act 1946 or under Part III of the National Assistance Act 1948, a hospital as defined in this Act, a police station, a mental nursing home or residential home for mentally disordered persons, or any other suitable place, the occupier of which is willing temporarily to receive the patient.

Mentally Disordered Persons Found in Public Places

Section 136.

This section *authorizes a constable to remove to a place of safety* an apparently mentally disordered person in immediate need of care or control, found by him in a place to which the public have access, *provided* he considers it necessary in the interests of that person or for the protection of other persons.

A person removed in this way may be detained in the *place of safety* for a period *not exceeding seventy-two hours* so that he may be examined by a medical practitioner and interviewed by an approved

140

social worker and any necessary arrangements made for his treatment or care.

Protection for Acts done in Pursuance of this Act

Section 139.

This section *protects persons from civil or criminal proceedings* in respect of any act purporting to be done in pursuance of the Act, regulations or rules *unless* the act was done in bad faith or without reasonable care. No civil proceedings may be brought without leave of the High Court and no criminal proceedings may be brought in any Court without the consent of the Director of Public Prosecutions. This section does *not* apply to proceedings against the Secretary of State or against a health authority within the meaning of the National Health Service Act 1979 (1977).

Notification of Hospitals Having Arrangements for Reception of Urgent Cases

Section 140.

This section *requires every Regional Health Authority and, in Wales, every District Health Authority to notify every local social services authority* for an area within the region or district *of the hospitals* in which there are arrangements for the reception *in case of special urgency of* patients requiring treatment for mental disorder.

Criminal Responsibility

The fact that a person is suffering from one of the forms of mental disorder described in the Mental Health Act 1983, whether or not he is subject to a hospital detention order or guardianship, is not of itself a defence to a criminal or civil charge. However, under the circumstances described in section 37, a Magistrate's Court may in the case of a person suffering from mental illness or severe mental impairment order his detention in hospital or reception into guardianship under the Act *without convicting him.* In other cases a mentally disordered person may be found *unfit to plead* because he is incapable of understanding the charge against him or instructing his counsel and in this case he is not put on trial but ordered to be detained until Her Majesty's pleasure be known.

If a mentally disordered person is fit to plead to a criminal charge he may be found *legally insane* if it can be shown that his mental disorder was at the time he committed the offence such that he did not know what he was doing or if he did, that he did not know that what he was doing was wrong (the so-called McNaghten rules). Upon finding a person legally insane, the Court orders him to be detained until Her Majesty's pleasure be known.

Contracts

A contract entered into by a *mentally impaired or severely mentally impaired person is binding upon him and upon the person contracting with him,* unless it can be shown that the former person was incapable of understanding the terms of the contract and the other person knew that his mental state was such that he did not understand what he was doing. If both these conditions are fulfilled, the contract entered into becomes voidable at the option of the mentally impaired or severely mentally impaired person or of his committee or trustees.

Testamentary Capacity

Legally, *the ability of the mentally impaired or severely mentally impaired person to execute a valid will is governed by the same conditions as in the case of the mentally ill.* Briefly, a will is valid only if the testator is able, at the time he makes it, to recall and keep clearly in his mind the nature and extent of his property and the persons who have claims on his bounty, his judgement and will being so unclouded as to enable him to determine the relative strength of these claims.

Marriage

There is no law to prevent the mentally impaired from marrying, but a marriage is voidable under the Matrimonial Causes Act 1950, if at the time of the marriage either of the parties was suffering from mental disorder within the meaning of the Mental Health Act 1983, of such a kind or to such an extent as to be unfitted for marriage and the procreation of children or subject to recurrent attacks of insanity or epilepsy, *provided* that the petitioner was at the time of the marriage ignorant of the facts alleged, that the proceedings were instituted *within a year* from the date of the marriage and that marital intercourse, with the consent of the petitioner, has not taken place since the discovery by the petitioner of the existence of the grounds for a decree. Mental disorder, of course, includes mental impairment or severe mental impairment.

Electoral Registration of Patients

Section 62 and Schedule 2 Mental Health (Amendment) Act 1982 *permit an informal patient aged 18 or over* who is a Commonwealth citizen or a citizen of the Republic of Ireland, *to register and vote in Parliamentary and local government elections, provided* he has made a declaration in the prescribed form, *without assistance,* by the qualifying date for inclusion in the electoral register. The person registered may vote if he applies to be treated as an absent voter for a particular election and furnishes an address in the United Kingdom to which the ballot paper is to be sent.

THE MENTAL HEALTH (AMENDMENT) (SCOTLAND) ACT 1983

The Scottish Amendment Act follows closely many of the amendments and additions to the Mental Health Act 1959 contained in the Mental Health Act 1983, but there are *a number of important differences* including, inter alia:

The definition of mental disorder still includes only two forms—mental illness and mental handicap (which replaces the former term 'mental deficiency'). The designation 'mental health officer' is retained in preference to 'approved social worker'. In general, the consent to treatment provision applies *only to detained patients.* Before giving his certificate under this section, the medical practitioner need consult *only one* other person 'who appears to him to be principally concerned with the case', and who is not otherwise specifically designated. On the other hand, a 'nurse of a prescribed class' is authorized to detain an informal patient for *only two hours* pending the arrival of a medical practitioner.

As the consolidated Mental Health (Scotland) Act 1983, with numbered sections, had not been published nor the operative date set at the time of going to press, the section on the Mental Health (Scotland) Act 1960 is reprinted without amendment.

THE MENTAL HEALTH (SCOTLAND) ACT, 1960

The provisions of the Mental Health (Scotland) Act 1960 differ from those of the Mental Health Act 1959, in the following main respects:

The numbering of sections dealing with similar provisions does not necessarily correspond in the two Acts.

PART I

Section 1 repeals the Lunacy (Scotland) Acts 1857 to 1913, and the Mental Deficiency (Scotland) Acts 1913 and 1940.

Section 2 establishes in place of the General Board of Control for Scotland, whose dissolution is effected by section 3:

THE MENTAL WELFARE COMMISSION FOR SCOTLAND

The Act requires that the Mental Welfare Commission shall consist of *no fewer than seven and not more than nine commissioners,* including its *Chairman.* It specifies that at least one commissioner shall be a *woman,* at least three shall be *medical practitioners,* and that one shall have been for a period of at least five years either a *Member of the Faculty of Advocates* or a *solicitor.*

The Commissioners are appointed by Her Majesty on the recommendation of the Secretary of State, and *members of the Civil Service are specifically barred* from membership of the Commission.

A *quorum* of the Mental Welfare Commission is defined as *four* Commissioners, including at least one medical commissioner.

Section 4.

This section *defines the functions and duties of the Mental Welfare Commission,* which include many of those formerly undertaken by the General Board of Control. Thus, the Mental Welfare Commission has the general function of protecting the persons and interest of those whose mental disorder prevents their doing so adequately themselves. For this purpose the Commission has *authority to discharge* such patients from detention in hospital or guardianship and a duty to enquire into any case where there may be ill-treatment, deficiency in care or treatment, or improper detention of a mentally disordered person, or a risk of loss or damage to his property. The Commission, represented by at least one medical member, is *required to visit regularly and to grant private interviews on request* to patients detained in hospital or subject to guardianship, and to draw the attention of the hospital board of management or local authority to any apparent shortcomings of the type specified above concerning any patient under their care.

Authority is imposed on the Commission to advise the Secretary of State on any matter arising out of the Act which he may refer to it and to draw his attention to any matter under the Act of which it feels he should be aware.

TYPES OF MENTAL DISORDER

Section 6.

This section *defines 'mental disorder'* as 'mental illness or mental deficiency however caused or manifested'. That is to say, the Mental Health (Scotland) Act 1960 recognizes only two types of mental disorder and retains the term 'mental deficiency' without defining it.

PART II

LOCAL AUTHORITY SERVICES

Functions of Local Health Authority:

* Section 7.

This section *authorizes the provision by local health authorities* of the same services for the mentally disordered as does Section 6 in the

*The local health authorities' responsibilities under this section were transferred to the local authorities' social service departments by the Social Work (Scotland) Act 1968.

Mental Health Act 1959, with the *exception* of specific mention of occupation and training facilities and with the *addition of the ascertainment of mental defectives* not of school age and the *supervision of mental defectives not subject to guardianship or detention in a hospital.* The description *'mental health officer'* replaces 'mental welfare officer'.

* Section 12.

This section *imposes a duty on local health authorities to provide,* or secure the provision of, suitable training and occupation, not only for children under the age of 16 years unsuitable for education or training in a special school, but also for mental defectives over that age, and to arrange the necessary transport.

Local Health Authority's Powers to compel attendance at Training Centres:

** Section 13.

This section corresponds, in effect to section 12, Mental Health Act 1959, with the exception that it is the Secretary of State who is required to reach a decision if the parent is aggrieved.

PART III

PRIVATE HOSPITALS AND RESIDENTIAL HOMES

Sections 15–18.

These sections differ from sections 14–17 in the Mental Health Act 1959, in that the premises are designated as *'private hospitals'* and not as 'mental nursing homes', and in that the functions of registration, imposition of conditions, and inspection are vested in the Secretary of State and not the local health authority.

PART IV

HOSPITAL CARE AND GUARDIANSHIP

It is in these sections that the Mental Health (Scotland) Act 1960 differs most significantly from the Mental Health Act 1959.

---

* The local health authorities' responsibilities under this section for children under 16 were transferred to the local authorities' education departments by the Education (Handicapped Children) Act 1970 and, for older mental defectives, to their social services departments by the Social Work (Scotland) Act 1968.

** See note on section 7.

Section 23.

This section, in effect, *excludes from compulsory admission to hospital* (except under the provisions for emergency admission) or *from reception into guardianship, patients over the age of 21 years,* who would satisfy the definitions of *subnormality* and *psychopathic disorder* in the Mental Health Act 1959. It imposes limitations (with exceptions) on the compulsory detention in hospital or under guardianship past the age of 25 years, of such patients, similar to the limitations in the latter Act.

Informal Admission of Patients to Hospital

Section 23 also *permits* the informal admission of mentally disordered patients *without* the mention of parental rights below the age of 16 years implied in section 5, Mental Health Act 1959.

COMPULSORY ADMISSION TO HOSPITAL AND RECEPTION INTO GUARDIANSHIP

Legal authority for detention in hospital or reception into guardianship is retained in the Mental Health (Scotland) Act 1960, in the person of the *Sheriff,* who has to approve all applications before they become effective.

There is no separate provision in the Mental Health (Scotland) Act 1960, for admission for *twenty-eight days' observation,* this, in effect, being incorporated in the procedure for the admission of patients to hospital for treatment.

Admission for Treatment

Section 24.

The *application for admission,* founded on *two medical recommendations,* has to be made by the nearest relative (defined in section 45) or by the mental health officer, who can act *in spite* of the nearest relative's objections (section 26), although he must inform him of his *right of appeal* to the Sheriff (section 28).

Section 27.

For the purposes of making their recommendations, the medical practitioners may examine the patient together only when no objection has been made by the patient or his nearest relative.

One of the medical practitioners has to be approved for the purposes of this section by the Regional Hospital Board, and not by the local health authority, as in the Mental Health Act 1959.

Not more than one of the medical recommendations may be given by a medical officer in the service of a local authority, and neither by a

146

medical practitioner who is making the application. The other exclusions listed in section 28, Mental Health Act 1959, do not apply, although the relationship of either medical practitioner to the patient, or any pecuniary interest he may have in the admission of the patient into hospital, has to be stated in his recommendation. Medical practitioners on the staff of a *private* hospital, or other private accommodation to which the patient is to be admitted, are specifically excluded from giving either medical recommendation.

Section 28.

The *application for admission* has to be submitted to the Sheriff for his approval *within seven days* of the last date on which the patient was examined for the purposes of any medical recommendation accompanying the application. The Sheriff, in considering the application, may make such enquiries and see such persons (including the patient) as he thinks fit. Where the patient's relative has objected to the application, he must afford that relative, and any witness the latter may call, an opportunity of being heard. At the patient's or applicant's request or the Sheriff's wish these proceedings shall be conducted in private.

Section 29.

The *Patient may be admitted* to the hospital named in the application at any time *within a period of seven days* from the date on which the Sheriff approved the application.

The board of management of the hospital are required to send to the Mental Welfare Commission, *within seven days* of the patient's admission, copies of the application and medical recommendations.

The *responsible medical officer* is required to examine the patient himself, or to obtain from another medical practitioner a report on the condition of the patient, *within the period of seven days ending on the twenty-eighth day after his admission.* If the responsible medical officer does not then discharge the patient, he must inform the Mental Welfare Commission, the nearest relative, and the board of management (cf. section 25, Mental Health Act 1959).

ADMISSION IN CASE OF EMERGENCY

Section 31.

This section *authorizes a medical practitioner,* who has personally examined a mentally disordered person, to make a medical recommendation concerning him *on the same day,* which permits the patient's removal to hospital *within three days* and his detention there *for a period not exceeding seven days provided* the medical practitioner considers the necessity for this is so urgent that compliance with the provisions of section 24 would involve unreasonable delay.

The medical practitioner is required, when practicable, to seek the consent of a relative or mental health officer to the making of an emergency recommendation, which must be accompanied by a statement that he has done so or of the reason for his failure to obtain that consent.

The board of management of the hospital to which the patient is admitted must, without delay, where practicable, inform the nearest relative and some responsible person residing with the patient of the latter's emergency admission.

APPLICATIONS IN RESPECT OF PATIENTS ALREADY IN HOSPITAL

Section 32.

This section *authorizes the use of the application for admission and emergency recommendation procedures for patients already in hospital,* and the latter procedure may therefore be used in an emergency to detain informal admissions pending action under section 24.

GUARDIANSHIP

*Section 25.

This section *authorizes,* subject to approval by the Sheriff of the application, the *reception into guardianship* of either a local health authority or of any other person (including the applicant himself) approved by that authority, or any person suffering from mental illness or mental deficiency which requires or is susceptible to medical treatment and warrants his reception into guardianship *provided* that this is in the interests of the patient or for the protection of other persons.

The same categories of patients are excluded by section 23 from liability to reception into guardianship as from liability to detention in hospital, and the same general provisions as to applications, reports to the Mental Welfare Commission and nearest relative, and medical recommendations apply to guardianship cases as to hospital cases.

The effect of a guardianship application, approved by the Sheriff and forwarded to the local health authority within seven days, is to confer on the authority or person named, to the exclusion of any other person, the same powers over the patient as would be the case if they or he were the father of the patient and the patient were a *pupil child.* However, the guardian is given no power with respect to any property of the patient and is prohibited from administering corporal punishment to him (section 29).

*See footnote on section 7.

148

LEAVE OF ABSENCE FROM HOSPITAL

Section 35.

There is no *automatic discharge* from hospital detention *after six months' authorized leave of absence* as in the Mental Health Act 1959, but the responsible medical officer is required *within fourteen days* to inform the Mental Welfare Commission of the patient's name and address on any leave *exceeding twenty-eight days,* including extensions of this duration of a previous six months' leave period. The responsible medical officer is also required to notify the commission *within fourteen days of the patient's return.*

ABSENCE WITHOUT LEAVE

Section 36.

The provisions of this section are similar to those of the Mental Health Act 1959, with the important variation in the period during which patients absent without leave, who are liable to detention in hospital or subject to guardianship, may be taken into custody, *i.e.,* in the case of a *mental defective—within three months,* in the case of a *patient subject to an emergency recommendation—within seven days,* and in *any other case—twenty-eight days,* beginning in each case with the first day of their absence.

TRANSFER OF PATIENTS

* Section 37.

A *patient may be transferred* from one hospital to another with the consent of the board of management of the two hospitals or from hospital to the guardianship of a local health authority or someone approved by the authority, with the consent of the board of management and the proposed guardian. A patient subject to guardianship may be transferred by a local health authority to the guardianship of another person with the latter's consent, but the Mental Welfare Commission's consent and that of the hospital board of management are required before a local authority can transfer a patient from guardianship to hospital and, in *all cases,* either the consent of the guardian must be obtained or, if this is refused, the approval of the Sheriff to the transfer must be sought. The board of management of the hospital to which the patient is transferred or the local health authority concerned, as the case may be, are required to notify the nearest relative and the Mental Welfare Commission *within seven days* of the date of transfer.

*See note on section 7.

DURATION OF AUTHORITY FOR DETENTION
OR GUARDIANSHIP AND DISCHARGE OF PATIENTS

Section 39.

The *initial duration and period of renewal* specified in this section are similar to those in section 43, Mental Health Act 1959, but in this case the responsible medical officer is required to obtain, *within two months of the expiry of authority,* for detention or guardianship, a report from *another* medical practitioner on the patient's condition, and to consider this report in assessing the need for continued detention or guardianship, having regard to their necessity in the interests of the health or safety of the patient and for the protection of other persons.

In each case where the responsible medical officer considers continued detention or guardianship necessary he is required to furnish a report to that effect, in the prescribed form, with the report of the second medical practitioner, to the board of management of the hospital or local health authority, as the case may be, and also to the Mental Welfare Commission.

The board of management or local health authority are required to notify the patient and his nearest relative or guardian when authority for detention or guardianship is renewed.

On *attaining the age of 16 years* a patient may appeal to the Sheriff to order his discharge, within the period for which the authority for his detention or guardianship is renewed.

Section 40.

This section *requires the responsible medical officer, board of management, or local health authority* to take action similar to that specified in section 39, *within two months of the 25th birthday* of a mental defective who has been continuously detained in hospital or subject to guardianship since attaining the age of 21 years, or of a patient detained in hospital or subject to guardianship who is suffering from mental illness which manifests itself only as persistent abnormally aggressive or seriously irresponsible conduct.

Where the authority for detention or guardianship is continued the patient and his nearest relative have, *within a period of twenty-eight days,* beginning with the patient's 25th birthday, the right of appeal to the Sheriff for the patient's discharge.

*See note on section 7.

DISCHARGE OF PATIENTS

*Section 43.

This section *authorizes the following persons to make an order discharging a patient from detention or guardianship:*

The *responsible medical officer* or the *Mental Welfare Commission* in the case of a patient detained in hospital or subject to guardianship (but not the responsible medical officer without the consent of the board of management when the patient is detained in a State hospital).

The *Sheriff* when an appeal has been made to him under sections 39, 40 or 44 of this Act.

The *nearest relative*, the *board of management*, in the case of a detained patient, and the *local health authority*, in the case of a patient subject to guardianship, with the consent in *both* cases of the responsible medical officer who, when he does not consent, is required to furnish a report that, in his opinion, the patient cannot be discharged without being a danger to himself or to others. In the absence of such a report the *discharge order takes effect at the end of a period of seven days after it is made.*

RESTRICTIONS ON DISCHARGE BY NEAREST RELATIVE

Section 44.

This section *requires the nearest relative to give not less than seven days' notice in writing* to the board of management or local health authority *of an order to discharge a patient* liable to detention in hospital or subject to guardianship and *authorizes the continued detention of the patient, against the nearest relative's wishes,* if the responsible medical officer reports to the appropriate authority, *within the period of notice,* that in his opinion the patient's mental disorder is such as would warrant his admission to hospital or reception into guardianship, or if the patient is already detained in hospital, that he would be likely to act in a manner dangerous to others or to himself, if discharged. It also *denies the relative the right to order discharge again during a period of six months* beginning with the date of the responsible medical officer's report, but requires the relative to be informed of the report and confers on the relative the *right to appeal to the Sheriff within the period of twenty-eight days,* beginning with the day on which he was informed.

This section also *precludes the nearest relative from making a discharge order in respect of a patient detained in a State hospital.*

*See note on section 7.

PART V

DETENTION OF PATIENTS CONCERNED IN CRIMINAL PROCEEDINGS AND TRANSFER OF PATIENTS UNDER SENTENCE

Section 54.

This section *authorizes a court,* when they are satisfied on the written or oral evidence of a medical practitioner, that a person charged with an offence whom they are remanding or committing for trial is suffering from mental disorder, *to commit him to hospital,* instead of remanding him in custody, *provided* the court is also satisfied that that hospital is available for his admission and suitable for his detention.

A person committed to hospital in this way is liable to be detained there for the period for which he is remanded or for the period of committal *unless,* before the expiration of that period, he is liberated in due course of law, or the responsible medical officer reports to the court that the person committed is not suffering from mental disorder of a nature or degree which warrants his admission to hospital under Part IV of the Act. In the latter case, the court may commit him to any prison or other institution to which he might have been committed had he not been committed to hospital, or may otherwise deal with him according to law.

* Section 55.

This section *authorizes the High Court of Judiciary or the Sheriff Court* (in the case of a person convicted of an offence other than an offence the sentence for which is fixed by law), or a Sheriff Court (in the case of a person remitted to that court by a court of summary jurisdiction other than a Sheriff Court, before which he has been charged with any act or omission constituting an offence punishable with imprisonment), *to order that person's admission to and detention in a specified hospital or to place him under the guardianship* of a local health authority provided that the court is satisfied, on the written or oral evidence of two medical practitioners, that the offender is suffering from mental disorder of a nature or degree which, in the case of a person *under 21 years of age,* would warrant his admission to a hospital or his reception into guardianship under Part IV of this Act and that, having regard to all the circumstances, this is the most suitable method of dealing with the case. The court must also be satisfied that the hospital specified will be able to admit the patient *within a period of twenty-eight days* beginning with the date of the making of the order, or that the local health authority or other person specified is willing to receive the offender into guardianship.

*See note on section 7.

152

A *Sheriff Court* may make an order under this section of the Act without convicting a person charged summarily before it *provided* the court is satisfied he did the act.

A *State hospital may not be specified* in a hospital order *unless* the court is satisfied, on the evidence of the medical practitioners, that the offender, on account of his dangerous, violent or criminal propensities, requires treatment under conditions of special security and cannot suitably be cared for in a hospital other than a State hospital.

A *duty is imposed on the prosecutor* to bring before the court evidence of the mental condition of any person charged who appears to him to be suffering from mental disorder.

*** *Section 56.*

This section *authorizes a Sheriff Court* (in the case of a child or young person brought before that court—or before a Juvenile Court and remitted to the Sheriff Court—under section 66 or section 68 of the Children and Young Persons (Scotland) Act 1937) *to make a hospital or guardianship order provided* the court is satisfied that the child or young person is in need of care and protection, or that his parent or guardian is unable to control him, and that the conditions which are required under section 55 for the making of a hospital order or guardianship order are, so far as applicable, satisfied in the case of the child or young person.

The court must also be satisfied that the *parent or guardian understands* the results which will follow from the order and *consents* to its being made.

A *duty is imposed on the person bringing the child or young person before the court* to bring such evidence as may be available of the mental condition of the child if he appears to that person to be suffering from mental disorder.

Section 58.

This section *cancels the power of the nearest relative to order discharge* of a patient admitted to hospital as a result of a court order and *removes*

*** Juvenile Courts have now been abolished in Scotland and the following procedure substituted by Part II of the Social Work (Scotland) Act 1968: an official with the title of 'Reporter' considers whether any child referred to him as having committed an offence is in need of compulsory measures of care and; if so, arranges for him to be brought with his parents before a 'Children's Hearing', which is a sitting of a treatment authority for each local authority area. The Children's Hearing has no power to adjudicate on whether or not the child committed the alleged offence and where the facts alleged are disputed, the hearing cannot proceed with the case unless it is referred to the Sheriff and he finds the facts established. The Children's Hearing then has the power to impose (by means of a 'supervision requirement') what compulsory measures of care it considers are required. For the purposes of the Act, 'child' means basically a person under 16 years of age but includes a person aged 16 and over but under 18 if he has a supervision requirement in force in respect of him.

the age limits to the detention in hospital or under guardianship of patients whose only manifestation of mental illness is persistent abnormally aggressive or irresponsible conduct, or whose mental deficiency is not such that they are incapable of living an independent life or of guarding themselves against serious exploitation.

Section 59.

This section *authorizes the patient's detention in a place of safety pending his admission to hospital within a period of twenty-eight days,* beginning with the day on which the hospital order was made by the court.

Section 60.

This section *authorizes a court making a hospital order to impose an order restricting the patient's discharge and any of the following special restrictions,* either indefinitely or for a specified period, where this is considered necessary for the protection of the public *provided* that the evidence of the medical practitioner approved by the Regional Hospital Board was given *orally* in Court: during the period that discharge is restricted, the normal limit to the duration of the authority for detention does not apply and a guardianship order may not be made in respect of the patient.

The *consent of the Secretary of State* is necessary before the patient can be transferred to another hospital or before he can be granted leave, and he can be recalled from leave at any time while the order restricting discharge is in force. The Secretary of State's consent is also necessary before the patient may be discharged by any of the persons who normally have this power.

Section 61.

This section *authorizes the Secretary of State to terminate the order restricting discharge* if he is satisfied that it is no longer required for the protection of the public. It also authorizes him, during the period of an order restricting discharge, to discharge the patient either absolutely or subject to conditions and, in the latter case, to recall him to hospital at any time while the order restricting discharge is still in force.

Section 62.

This section *gives a patient a right of appeal against a hospital or guardianship order or order restricting discharge made by a court.*

Section 65.

This section *authorizes the Secretary of State to apply to the Sheriff to direct the transfer of a person in custody, awaiting trial or sentence, to a hospital* (*not* a private hospital), when it appears to the Secretary of

State that the person is suffering from mental disorder of a nature or degree which warrants his admission to a hospital under Part IV of the Act. If the Sheriff is satisfied of this, on the reports of *two* medical practitioners, he may make a hospital order, which is *subject to a restriction on discharge of unlimited duration. At least one* of the medical practitioners giving reports must be approved by the Regional Hospital Board* as having special experience in the diagnosis or treatment of mental disorders. Each medical practitioner must describe the patient as suffering from the *same* one form of mental disorder, although either, or both, may describe him as suffering from the other form as well. A detention order under this section is *valid for a period of fourteen days* beginning with the date on which it is given.

The patient remains liable to be detained in hospital, *but not subject to a restriction order,* if the proceedings against him are dropped, or after his case has been disposed of by the Court to which he was committed or by which he was remanded, unless the Court pass a sentence of imprisonment or make a guardianship order concerning him, or the responsible medical officer notifies the Secretary of State that he no longer requires treatment for mental disorder (section 68).

Section 66.

This section *authorizes the Secretary of State,* if he is satisfied on similar reports to those required under section 65 that a person is suffering from mental disorder which warrants his admission to hospital, *to direct that person's transfer to hospital from prison* in which he is serving a sentence as a civil prisoner or detained as an alien. This direction is *valid for a period of fourteen days* beginning with the date on which it is given.

A person dealt with in this way may appeal to the Sheriff within three months, and if his transfer order is cancelled the Secretary of State is required to direct his return to prison.

Section 67.

This section *authorizes the Secretary of State to impose restriction on discharge of prisoners transferred to hospital.*

Section 69.

This section *authorizes the Secretary of State to direct the transfer back to prison* of any patient subject to a direction restricting his discharge, on notification by the responsible medical officer that he no longer requires treatment for mental disorder *provided the period of his prison sentence has not expired.*

*Now Regional Health Authority

The responsible medical officer is required to assess the need for the continued detention of a patient *after a direction restricting his discharge has ceased to have effect,* on the basis of a report on his condition obtained by the responsible medical officer from *another* medical practitioner *within a period of twenty-eight days of the expiry of that order.* If the responsible medical officer considers that the patient's continued detention in hospital is necessary in the interests of the health or safety of the patient or for the protection of other persons, he is required to furnish a report to this effect, in the prescribed form, with the other medical practitioner's report, to the hospital board of management and Mental Welfare Commission. The patient is then treated as though he had been admitted to hospital on a hospital order *without restriction on his discharge* on the date the previous restriction direction expired, and the patient and his nearest relative must be informed of this by the board of management.

* *Section 71.*

This section *authorizes the Secretary of State to direct that a child or young person detained in an approved school be placed under the guardianship of a local health authority,* if he is satisfied on the reports required under section 65 that the child or young person is suffering from mental disorder of a nature or degree which warrants his reception into guardianship under this Act and that this is in the public interest.

PART VI

REMOVAL AND RETURN OF PATIENTS WITHIN THE UNITED KINGDOM, ETC.

Sections 73–88.

These sections, with the amendments they contain to the Mental Health Act 1959, *authorize the Secretary of State/Minister of Health to direct the transfer of a patient liable to be detained or subject to guardianship in Scotland, England, Wales or Northern Ireland to any other of these countries if* he considers this to be in the patient's interest.

The sections similarly *authorize the taking into custody* anywhere within Scotland, England, Wales or Northern Ireland of any patient absent without leave.

PART VIII

STATE HOSPITALS

The State hospitals in Scotland correspond to the *special hospitals* in England.

* See note on section 7.

Section 89.
This section requires *the Secretary of State to provide State hospitals* for mentally disordered patients subject to detention who require treatment under conditions of special security on account of their dangerous, violent, or criminal propensities.

MISCELLANEOUS AND GENERAL

PATIENTS' CORRESPONDENCE

Section 34.
This section differs from section 36, Mental Health Act 1959, only in the following list of persons which is substituted for that in the latter section:

1. The nearest relative of the patient
2. The Secretary of State
3. The Lord Advocate
4. Any Member of the Commons House of Parliament
5. Any Mental Welfare Commission or any Commissioner thereof
6. Any Sheriff or Sheriff Clerk
7. The board of management of the hospital

ILL-TREATMENT OF PATIENTS

Section 95.
As section 126, Mental Health Act 1959, except that it specifies the amount of the maximum possible fine as £500 on conviction on indictment.

SEXUAL INTERCOURSE WITH FEMALE DEFECTIVES

Section 96.
This section *renders it an offence for a man to have unlawful sexual intercourse with a female defective,* for anyone to procure or encourage a female defective to have unlawful sexual intercourse, or for the owner or occupier of any premises or any person having or assisting in the management or control of the premises to induce a female defective to resort to or be on such premises for the purpose of unlawful sexual intercourse with any man *provided* these persons had reason to know or had reason to suspect that the woman concerned was a defective incapable of living an independent life or of guarding herself against serious exploitation. The penalty for the above offence is, on conviction on indictment, a term of imprisonment not exceeding two years.

Section 97.

This section, which *concerns sexual intercourse with patients,* is in all essential respects identical with section 128, Mental Health Act 1959, except that the institution of proceedings is not dependent on the consent of the Director of Public Prosecutions.

ASSISTING PATIENTS TO ABSENT THEMSELVES WITHOUT LEAVE

Section 98.

As section 129, Mental Health Act 1959, except that it specifies the amount of the maximum possible fine as £500 on conviction on indictment.

AUTHORITY TO SEARCH FOR AND REMOVE PATIENTS

Section 103.

This section *authorizes a mental health officer or medical commissioner,* on production of documentary proof of his authority, to demand admission at all reasonable times to inspect any place in which he has reasonable cause to believe that a person suffering from mental disorder is being ill-treated, neglected, or not kept under proper control, or is living alone and unable to care for himself. When a Justice of the Peace, on sworn evidence in writing by either of these officers, is satisfied that he has been refused admission, or such refusal is apprehended, the *Justice may issue a warrant authorizing a constable to enter,* if need be by force, any premises specified in the warrant, and, if thought fit, *to remove any person suffering from mental disorder from there to a place of safety,* pending arrangements for his treatment or care. The constable *must* be accompanied in the execution of the warrant by a medical practitioner.

This section also authorizes a Justice of the Peace, on the sworn evidence in writing of any constable or any other person authorized under the Act (or under section 93, Mental Health Act 1959) to take a patient to any place or to take into custody or retake a patient, *to issue a warrant authorizing any named constable to enter any premises,* if need be by force, and *to remove from there any patient liable to be taken or retaken provided* admission to the premises has been refused or if such a refusal is apprehended. The constable *may* be accompanied in the execution of the warrant by a *medical practitioner* or by *any person authorized* under the Act (or section 93, Mental Health Act 1959) to take or retake the patient.

A patient removed to a place of safety under this section may be detained there for a period *not exceeding seventy-two hours.*

A *place of safety* means a hospital as defined by this Act, a residential home for persons suffering from mental disorder, or any other suitable place, the occupier of which is willing temporarily to receive the patient, but shall *not* include a police station unless by reason of emergency there is no place as aforesaid available for receiving the patient.

MENTALLY DISORDERED PERSONS FOUND IN PUBLIC PLACES

Section 104.

As section 136, Mental Health Act 1959, with the omission of the interview by a mental welfare officer, but with the *additional requirement* that the constable inform *without delay* some responsible person residing with the patient and the nearest relative of the patient.

NORTHERN IRELAND

At the time of going to press, the Committee of the Department of Health and Social Services had not yet completed the draft of the proposed new legislation and it is anticipated that it may be another year before the Bill is submitted for debate. The section on the Act is, therefore, reprinted from the last edition, but in an expanded form.

THE MENTAL HEALTH ACT (NORTHERN IRELAND) 1961

The Mental Health Act (Northern Ireland) 1961 differs considerably from the Mental Health Act 1959 and from the Mental Health (Scotland) Act 1960 as regards definitions and the procedures for hospital detention and guardianship.

As a result of the reorganization of Health and Social Services which took place in Northern Ireland on 1st October 1972, the only fully integrated service for the mentally handicapped in the British Isles was unfortunately destroyed by the abolition of the Northern Ireland Hospitals Authority which had previously been responsible for both hospital and community care. Also abolished were its three special care management committees, whose duties included the ascertainment of persons requiring special care, their supervision, guardianship and training in the community and in residential accommodation, including hospitals. These duties are now the responsibility of four Area Boards for Health and Social Services and references in the following Section of the Act to the Authority or Management Committee should be amended accordingly.

PART I

Sections 1 to 4 define the general duties and powers of the Northern Ireland Hospitals Authority and their specific duty to submit to the Ministry of Health and Local Government schemes for the management and control of special care services, and the Ministry's duty to implement schemes it has approved (with or without modifications).

Section 6.

This section *permits* the informal admission to any hospital or private hospital of any person who requires treatment for mental disorder and also permits such a person to make use of any of the services provided under the Act for persons requiring special care. By inference from subsection 2 of this section, a patient informally admitted may be detained in hospital at his parent's or guardian's request until the age of 16, whatever his own wishes in the matter may be, but on reaching the age of 16 years, if he is capable of expressing his own wishes, these override those of his parent or guardian.

Section 7.

This *section defines mental disorder as mental illness, arrested or incomplete development of mind and any other disorder or disability of mind.* It *defines* also *a person requiring special care as someone suffering from arrested or incomplete development of mind,* (whether arising from inherent causes or induced by disease or injury) *which renders him socially inefficient to such an extent that he requires supervision, training or control in his own interests or in the interests of other persons. The criteria of social inefficiency are defined as incapability of guarding oneself against physical dangers, managing oneself or one's affairs or, if a child, of being taught to do so or being found unsuitable for education at school, or whether a child or adult, being in need of care for the protection of other persons.*

PART II

PROVISIONS RELATING TO SPECIAL CARE AND ADMISSION TO HOSPITAL AND GUARDIANSHIP

Notification and Examination of Persons Requiring Special Care

Section 8.

This section *imposes a duty* on any medical practitioner, health authority or welfare authority *to notify* to the local education authority any person between the ages of 2 and 16, and to the special care management committee, any other case where it appears that steps should be taken, either in the interests of the person concerned or for the protection of other persons, *to ascertain* whether he is a person requiring special care.

On receiving such a notification, the local education authority or special care management committee, is required to notify the nearest relative where the person is under the age of 16 years, or the person himself and his nearest relative if he is over that age.

Section 9.

This section *authorizes special care management committees to require,* by notice in writing, *persons notified* under section 8 of this Act or sections 32 or 53 of the Education Act (Northern Ireland) 1947, *to submit themselves for examination by a medical practitioner* appointed by the authority for the purposes of section 19, where such an examination has not taken place or been arranged by the person concerned (or by his nearest relative if he is under the age of 16) after the date of notification.

This section also *gives special care management committees similar powers to require medical examination of persons* ordinarily resident within their area, *who appear to them to require special care,* and entitles the nearest relative to be present at any medical examination of which he has been notified in the case of a person under the age of 16 years.

Attendance at Training Centres of Children Requiring Special Care

Section 10.

This section *gives any special care committee powers,* on giving notice in writing to the parent of a child of compulsory school age, *to compel the parent to cause the child to attend a training centre* provided or approved by the Authority, either by day or as a resident, where it appears to the committee that the child should receive such training and that he is not receiving adequate comparable training elsewhere. Where a notified parent feels aggrieved on the ground that the child is receiving such training, he may require the special care committee to refer the question to the *Review Tribunal,* who may either confirm the notice or direct its amendment or withdrawal.

Section 11.

This section lists the following *'reasonable causes'* for exemptions in respect of section 10:

sickness of the child preventing his attendance at the centre
non-attendance on any day exclusively set apart for religious observance by the religious body to which the person notified belongs

impracticability for the child to make his own way or to be taken to and from the centre, in the absence of suitable arrangements for his transport or residential accommodation at or near the centre, by the special care management committee

the child's lack of a fixed abode, due to the nature of his parents' business, provided the child has attended as regularly as the latter permits

other circumstances which in the opinion of the Authority or the court afford a reasonable excuse.

Admission to Hospital

Section 12.

This section *authorizes,* as the result of an application for admission, the *detention in hospital for a period not exceeding twenty-one days,* of any person suffering from mental illness or requiring special care *provided* it can be shown that his mental disorder warrants this and that it is in the interests of his own health or of the protection of others.

The application has to be founded on the *written recommendation* in the prescribed form, signed on or before the date of application, *of one medical practitioner,* who has personally examined the patient not more than two days before the date on which he signs the recommendation, and who, if practicable, shall be the patient's medical practitioner, or by a medical practitioner who has previous acquaintance with the patient (section 14).

The medical recommendation must confirm that the above conditions concerning the mental disorder are satisfied and state the grounds for that opinion and whether other methods of dealing with the patient are available and, if so, why they are not appropriate.

Section 14 *excludes* the following persons from giving the recommendation:

a. the applicant;
b. a partner of the applicant;
c. a person employed as an assistant by the applicant;
d. a person who receives or has an interest in the receipt of any payments made on account of the maintenance of the patient; or
e. except in the case of an emergency application (as defined in section 15), a practitioner on the staff of the hospital to which the patient is to be admitted; or by the husband, wife, father, father-in-law, mother, mother-in-law, son, son-in-law, daughter, daughter-in-law, brother, brother-in-law, sister or sister-in-law of the patient.

Section 13.

An *application for admission* may be made either *by the nearest relative* (as defined by section 37) or *by the welfare officer* for the area in which the patient then is, after consultation with the nearest relative (and *not against his expressed objection*), unless consultation is not reasonably practicable or would involve unreasonable delay. The applicant must personally have seen the patient within a period of fourteen days ending with the date of the application.

The patient must be admitted to hospital within a period of fourteen days beginning with the date on which he was examined by the medical practitioner giving the recommendation for admission (section 17).

The patient may apply to the *Review Tribunal* within the period of six months beginning with the day on which he was admitted to hospital or with the day on which he attains the age of 16 years, whichever is the later (section 19).

Admission in Case of Emergency

Section 15.

This section authorizes the *welfare officer* or *any relative of the patient,* in any case of urgent necessity, to apply for the patient's detention in hospital if full compliance with the provisions of section 12 would involve undesirable delay. The application may be founded on one medical recommendation only.

The patient must be admitted to hospital within a period of three days beginning with the date on which he was examined by the medical practitioner giving the recommendation for admission (section 17).

Under this emergency procedure, the *patient may be detained for seven days only,* beginning with the day on which he was admitted to hospital, unless the management committee of the hospital receive the medical report mentioned in section 19, within that period.

Applications in Respect of Patients already in Hospital

Section 16.

This section *authorizes the detention in hospital for a period of three days of an informal admission,* on the written report to the management committee by the *medical practitioner in charge of treatment,* that it appears to him that an application should be made for the patient's admission to hospital and his detention there.

Section 18.

This section *requires a medical practitioner on the staff of the hospital to which a patient is admitted for treatment, to examine him immediately after admission* (unless he has been examined before admission by a medical practitioner appointed for the purposes of section 19) and to report the results in writing to the management committee.

Section 19.

This section *extends the authority for detention in hospital* of a patient admitted under section 12 *for a period of up to six months* beginning with the day on which he was so admitted, *provided a* medical officer appointed by the Authority for the purpose of this section makes a medical report to the management committee in the prescribed form, between the fourteenth and twenty-first day after admission, that, in his opinion, the patient is suffering from mental disorder of a nature or degree which warrants his detention in hospital, and that this is necessary in the interests of his own health or safety or for the protection of other persons, with a statement of the grounds for his opinion and the reasons why other methods of dealing with the patient are not appropriate.

The following are prohibited from giving a medical report under this section—the person making the application for admission of the patient, the medical officer who gave the recommendation for admission, or a person who receives or has an interest in the receipt of payments made on account of the maintenance of the patient, or by the husband, wife, father, father-in-law, mother, mother-in-law, son, son-in-law, daughter, daughter-in-law, sister or sister-in-law of the patient.

The medical report has no effect unless both it and the recommendation for admission describe the patient as being mentally ill or as requiring special care (whether or not they describe the patient in both those ways).

GUARDIANSHIP

Section 21.

This section *authorizes the reception into guardianship* of either a local authority, a management committee or any other person including the applicant himself, approved by the management committee, of any person suffering from mental illness or requiring special care, which warrants his reception into guardianship, *provided* that it is necessary in his own interest or for the protection of other persons.

The *guardianship application* is founded on the *written recommendations* in the prescribed form *of two medical practitioners* who have each examined the patient not more than two days before the date on which each signs the recommendation. *One recommendation must be given by a medical practitioner appointed by the Authority for the purposes of section 19* and the other, if practicable, by the patient's medical practitioner or by a practitioner with previous acquaintance with the patient. The recommendations may be signed separately or given as a joint recommendation signed by both medical practitioners. The recommendations must state the grounds and reasons for the medical

164

practitioners' opinion and include a statement why other methods of dealing with the patient are not appropriate.

Section 22.

A guardianship application accepted by a management committee itself or on behalf of another named individual, confers on that committee or person all such powers in relation to the patient as would be exercisable by the father of a child under the age of 14 years.

The guardianship application must be forwarded to the management committee within fourteen days beginning with the date on which the patient was last examined by a medical practitioner before giving a recommendation for guardianship.

A patient placed under guardianship may be kept under guardianship for a period not exceeding six months beginning with the day on which the guardianship application was accepted, but the patient may apply to the *Review Tribunal* within that period or within a period of six months of his 16th birthday, whichever is the later.

Section 23.

This section defines the procedure for transfer of guardianship in the event of the death or incapacity of the guardian or of the neglect by him of his duties towards the patient.

Section 24.

This section requires the guardian, as far as is practicable, to make arrangements for the occupation, training or employment of the patient and for his recreational and general welfare, including the promotion of his physical and mental health.

Patients' Correspondence

Section 25.

This section requires the management committee, a person carrying on a private hospital, or a person appointed as a guardian *to forward unopened* all letters addressed by any patient liable to be detained or subject to guardianship to the following:

the Lord Chief Justice
the Minister of Health and Local Government
any member of Parliament
the Review Tribunal
the Ministry
the Registrar of the Department for the Affairs of Mental Patients
the nearest relative of the patient

Rights of Patients and Nearest Relatives

Section 27.

This section requires management committees to furnish the patient and his nearest relative with a *statement of their respective rights* and powers under the Act, as soon as practicable after the patient is admitted to hospital or placed under guardianship.

Reclassification of Mental Disorder

Section 28.

This section authorizes the *reclassification of the form of mental disorder,* where the responsible medical officer (as defined in section 47) reports to the management committee or to the guardian that the patient is suffering from a form of mental disorder other than that specified in the original application, and requires the management committee or guardian to inform the patient himself if he is over the age of 16 and his nearest relative of the report. The patient, or his nearest relative, may apply to the *Review Tribunal* within twenty-eight days beginning with the day on which he was so informed.

Leave of Absence from Hospital

Section 29.

This section *authorizes the responsible medical officer to grant, for any period, leave of absence* to a patient detained in hospital, subject to any condition he considers necessary in the interests of the patient or for the protection of other persons, including the requirement that the patient shall remain during his absence in the custody of any person authorized in writing by the management committee. The responsible medical officer may *revoke the leave* of absence and recall the patient to hospital if it appears necessary to do so in the interests of the patient's health or safety or for the protection of other persons or because the patient is not receiving proper care.

Absence Without Leave

Section 30.

This section *authorizes the taking into custody and the return to hospital* by any officer on the staff of the hospital, any welfare officer, any constable or any person authorized in writing by the management committee of the hospital, of any patient absent without leave from hospital or failing to return to the hospital at the expiration of a period of authorized leave, or, if recalled from leave or absconding himself without permission from any place where he is required to reside as a condition of leave.

Similarly, this section *authorizes the taking into custody and return to his required place of residence* by any officer on the staff of a management committee, by any constable or any person authorized in writing by the guardian or a management committee, of any patient subject to guardianship, who absents himself without the leave of his guardian from his required place of residence.

A *patient may not be taken into custody after the expiration of twenty-eight days beginning with the first day of his absence without leave,* and after this period he ceases to be liable to be detained or subject to guardianship.

Transfer of Patients

Section 31.
This section authorizes the continued detention of patients liable to detention, when they are transferred by the Authority from one hospital to another, the transfer of a detained patient from hospital to guardianship of any person by arrangement of the management committee, the transfer of a patient already subject to guardianship to the guardianship of any other person or to a hospital, in each case by arrangement of the same committee.

A patient who has attained the age of 16 years, transferred from guardianship to hospital in this way, may apply to the *Review Tribunal* within the period of six months beginning with the day on which he is transferred.

Renewal of Authority for Detention or Guardianship

Section 32.
This section *extends the authority for detention in hospital or guardianship for a further period of one year* from the expiry of the six months period specified in sections 19 and 22, *if* within a period of one month ending with the last day of that period, the responsible medical officer examines the patient and reports to the responsible management committee in the prescribed form that continued detention or guardianship is necessary in the interests of the patient's health or safety or for the protection of other persons.

The section *extends the same authority for a further period of two years* from the expiry of the first extension of one year, *if* within a period of two months, ending with the last day of that period, two medical practitioners have, by arrangement of the management committee, examined the patient and reported in writing, either separately or jointly, to the responsible management committee in the prescribed form, that in the practitioners' opinion the requirements of sections 12 and 21 as regards the patient's condition and the inappropriateness of alternative methods of care for him are satisfied. The management committee is

167

required to give the patient and his nearest relative not less than fourteen days' notice in writing of the date of the medical examination. At least one of the medical practitioners appointed to carry out the examination must have made neither the original recommendation for admission or guardianship nor the medical report in connection with the detention of the patient.

The section *extends the same authority subsequently for periods of two years at a time* from the expiry of the preceding period, *if* within a period of two months ending with the last day of each two year period, the responsible medical officer examines the patient and reports to the responsible management committee in the prescribed form that continued detention or guardianship is necessary in the interests of the patient's health or safety or for the protection of other persons.

This section requires the responsible management committee to inform in writing a patient who has attained the age of 16 years, of the renewal of the authority for his detention or guardianship, and the patient may apply to the *Review Tribunal* at any time before the expiry of the period of renewal.

Discharge of Patients

Section 35.

This section *authorizes the following persons to make an order in writing discharging a patient from detention or guardianship* (referred to as '*an order for discharge*')—the responsible medical officer, the responsible management committee or the nearest relative—and the responsible medical officer is required to make such an order if he is satisfied that the patient no longer suffers from mental disorder and that, having regard to the care or supervision available if he were discharged, it is not necessary in the interests of his health or safety, or for the protection of other persons for him to continue to be liable to detention or subject to guardianship. Except where the patient is discharged from hospital other than on the application of his nearest relative, the responsible medical officer is required to notify the appropriate welfare authority to that effect.

The responsible medical officer is prohibited from discharging a patient detained in any special accommodation without the consent of the management committee.

Restrictions on Discharge by the Nearest Relative

Section 36.

This section *requires the nearest relative to give not less than seventy two hours notice in writing of an order for discharge* (extended to ninety-six hours if that period includes a Sunday) to the management committee of the hospital and *authorizes the continued detention of the*

168

patient, against the nearest relative's wishes, if the responsible medical officer reports in writing to the management committee that, in his opinion, *the patient would be likely to act in a manner dangerous to others or to himself if discharged,* and that he is not satisfied that the patient would receive proper treatment.

The section also *denies the relative the right to order discharge again during a period of six months* beginning with the day of the responsible medical officer's report, but requires the relative to be informed of the report and confers on him the right to apply to the *Review Tribunal* within a period of twenty-eight days beginning with the day on which he was informed.

Reference of Cases to the Review Tribunal

Section 45.

This section authorizes the following persons to refer the case of any patient liable to be detained or subject to guardianship to the Review Tribunal at any time—the Attorney General, the Ministry or, on the direction of the Lord Chief Justice, the Registrar of the Affairs of Mental Patients.

Definition of Responsible Medical Officer

Section 47.

This section *defines the responsible medical officer* 'as any medical practitioner authorized to act as responsible medical officer by the Authority in the case of a patient detained in hospital, or by the management committee in the case of a patient subject to guardianship'.

PART III

ADMISSION OF PATIENTS CONCERNED IN CRIMINAL PROCEEDINGS AND TRANSFER OF PATIENTS UNDER SENTENCE

Section 48.

This section *authorizes a Court of Assize or Quarter Sessions* (in the case of a person convicted of an offence other than one for which the sentence is fixed by law) or *a Court of Summary Jurisdiction* (in the case of a person convicted of an offence punishable with imprisonment on summary conviction) *to order that person to be committed to the care of the Authority for admission to hospital or to place him under guardianship of a management committee,* or of any other specified person approved by a management committee, *provided* that the Court is satisfied on the written or oral evidence of the medical practitioners (of whom at least one shall be approved by the Authority for the purposes of section 19, (section 50)) that the offender is suffering from mental disorder of a nature or degree which would warrant his detention under Part II, and that having regard to all the circumstances, this is the most suitable method of dealing with the case.

A *Court of Summary Jurisdiction may make an order* under this section *without convicting* a person if the Court is satisfied he did the act and the other requirements of this section are satisfied.

The Court is required to be satisfied that the person to be named in a guardianship order is willing to receive the patient into guardianship.

Section 49.

This section *authorizes a Juvenile Court* (in the case of a child or young person brought before the Court under section 63 or section 65 of the Children's and Young Persons' Act (Northern Ireland) 1950) *to make a hospital order or guardianship order, provided* that the Court is satisfied that the child or young person is in need of care or protection, or that his parent or guardian is unable to control him and that the conditions which are required under section 48 for the making of a hospital or guardianship order are, so far as is applicable, satisfied in the case of the child or young person.

The Court must also be satisfied that *the parent or guardian understands* the results which will follow from the order and consents to its being made.

Section 50.

This section *requires that a copy of any medical report tendered in evidence to the Court* in connection with sections 48 or 49 *is given to the accused's counsel or solicitor,* or if the accused is not legally represented, requires that the contents of the report shall be disclosed to him, or, if he is a child or young person, to his parents or guardian if present in Court, except in each case where the report has been tendered in evidence on his behalf.

In any case the accused may require that the practitioner by whom the report was signed be called to give oral evidence and rebutting evidence may be called by him or on his behalf.

Section 51.

This section *imposes a duty on the Authority to designate a hospital to which a patient subject to a hospital order may be taken* by a constable, welfare officer or any other person directed by the Court, and *imposes a duty on the management committee of that hospital to admit him* within a period of twenty-eight days.

This section also *cancels the powers of the nearest relative* under section 35 *to order the discharge of a patient admitted to hospital as the*

170

result of a Court order. However, it authorizes the patient to apply to the *Review Tribunal* within the period of six months beginning with the date of the order or the day on which he attains the age of 16 years, whichever is the later, and authorizes the nearest relative to make a similar application within the period of twelve months beginning with the date of the order, and in any subsequent period of twelve months.

Section 52.

This section *authorizes the patient's detention in a place of safety pending his admission to hospital* within the period of twenty-eight days beginning with the day on which the hospital order was made by the Court.

Powers of Court to Restrict Discharge from Hospital

Section 53.

This section *authorizes a Court to impose an order restricting the patient's discharge and any of the following restrictions, either indefinitely or for a specified period,* where, having regard to the nature of the offence, this is considered necessary for the protection of the public, *provided* that the medical practitioners appointed by the Authority for the purposes of section 19 have given evidence orally in Court:

During the period that discharge is restricted, the normal limit to the duration of the authority for detention does not apply and no application can be made to the Review Tribunal.

The consent of the Minister of Home Affairs is necessary before the patient can be transferred to another hospital or to guardianship or vice versa or before he can be granted leave, and he can be recalled from leave by the Minister as well as by the responsible medical officer while the order restricting discharge is in force.

Section 54.

This section *authorizes the Minister of Home Affairs himself, and no one else, to terminate the order restricting discharge.* While the order restricting discharge is still in force, the Minister may discharge the patient from hospital either absolutely or subject to conditions, with power to recall the patient to hospital if he thinks this necessary.

Under this section, *a patient subject to an order restricting his discharge is entitled,* within the period of six months beginning with the date of the relevant hospital order or with the day on which he attains the age of 16 years, whichever is later, and within each period during which he could himself have made an application to the Review Tribunal if the restriction order had not been in force, *to request the Minister to refer his case to the Review Tribunal for their advice. The Minister is required to comply with this request within two months of receiving it.* A patient recalled to hospital after being conditionally discharged may, in addition, make a similar request to the Minister during the period six to twelve months from the date of his return to hospital.

Appeals

Section 55.

This section *authorizes a patient subject to a hospital or guardianship order or order restricting his discharge made by a Court of Summary Jurisdiction* (whether or not the Court convicted him), *County Court, or Court of Assize, to appeal against the order* in the same manner as against a conviction.

Transfer to Hospital or Guardianship of Prisoners, etc.

Section 58.

This section *authorizes the Minister to direct the transfer of a person serving a prison sentence to hospital if* he is satisfied on the reports of at least two medical practitioners that the person is suffering from mental illness or requires special care which warrants his detention in hospital for medical treatment and that this is in the public interest. At least one of the medical practitioners giving reports must be approved for the purposes of section 19 by the Authority. Each medical practitioner must describe the patient as being mentally ill or as requiring special care, although either or both may describe him as suffering from both forms of mental disorder.

Section 59.

This section *authorizes the Minister,* if he is satisfied on similar reports to those required under section 58 that a person is suffering from mental illness or requires special care which warrants his detention in hospital for medical treatment, *to order that person's transfer to hospital from the various types of custody specified in the section* or from civil imprisonment or from detention in prison as an alien. The restrictions of section 53 are applied mandatorily to all but the last two categories of prisoners, to whom they may be applied at the discretion of the Minister (section 60).

Section 61.

This section *authorizes the Minister to direct the transfer back to prison or any other institution of detention, any patient subject to an order restricting his discharge,* on notification by the responsible medical officer that he no longer requires treatment for mental disorder, *provided* the period of his prison sentence has not expired. Under this section the Minister may himself exercise, or authorize the managers of a training school to which a patient might have been remitted, to exercise any power of releasing him on licence or discharging him under supervision which would have been exercizable if he had been remitted to a prison or other institution of detention.

Section 62.

This section *authorizes the Minister to direct that a person on remand, who is subject to a hospital transfer direction, be transferred to a place where he would otherwise have been detained* if he had not been committed to the care of the Authority, *provided* the responsible medical officer notifies the Minister that he no longer requires treatment for mental disorder.

This section also *authorizes a Court of Assize or a County Court to make a hospital order* (with or without an order restricting discharge) *concerning a person in his absence, if* the Court is satisfied on the medical evidence of at least two medical practitioners (at least one of whom must be a practitioner appointed by the Authority for the purposes of section 19) that the person is suffering from mental disorder of a nature or degree which warrants his detention in hospital for medical treatment, and if the Court is satisfied that it is impracticable or inappropriate to bring him before the Court. The Court must be further satisfied after considering any depositions or other documents required to be sent to the proper officer of the Court that it is proper for it to make such an order.

Section 63.

This section *gives similar authority to that in section 62 to a Court of Summary Jurisdiction to make a hospital order* (with or without an order restricting discharge) *concerning a person in custody on remand, in his absence and without convicting* him, *provided* that it appears impracticable or inappropriate to bring him before the Court and that the conditions required by section 62 concerning medical and other evidence are satisfied.

Section 65.

This section *authorizes the Minister to direct that a child or young person detained in a training school be placed under the guardianship of a management committee or* any such other person approved by a management committee subject to the willingness of either to accept him, if he is satisfied on the reports required under section 58 that the child or young person is suffering from mental disorder which warrants his reception into guardianship under this Act and that it is in the public interest and expedient to do so.

173

PART IV

REGISTRATION OF PRIVATE HOSPITALS

Sections 67 to 72 concern the conditions of registration of private hospitals by the Ministry and the control of private hospitals by those running them and by regular inspection on behalf of the Minister.

PART V

PROPERTY OF PATIENTS

Section 73.

This section *requires a* welfare authority to apply to the Department of Affairs of Mental Patients for the appointment of a committee in respect of the estate of any person in their area who is incapable by reason of mental disorder of managing his affairs.

Section 74.

This section *requires management committees, welfare authorities and persons running private hospitals to notify the Department for the Affairs of Mental Patients, of any person under their care* whom they have reason to believe is *incapable of managing his affairs* by reason of mental disorder, within such time and in such form as the Lord Chief Justice may prescribe.

Section 75.

This section *authorizes the authority* responsible for the payment of earnings or pension from the sources referred to in the section to any person incapable by reason of mental disorder of managing and administering his property and affairs, *to pay whatever proportion they think fit to the institution or person having the care of the patient, to be applied for his benefit.* At their discretion they may pay all or part of the remainder to members of the patient's family or other persons for whom the patient might be expected to provide if he were not mentally disordered, or in reimbursements of money applied by any person in payment of the patient's debts or his maintenance or other benefit or that of his dependants referred to above, provided in each case that a committee, receiver or guardian has not been appointed in Northern Ireland in respect of the patient's estate.

PART VI

THE REVIEW TRIBUNAL

There is only one Review Tribunal for Northern Ireland with membership and functions similar to those of the Mental Health Review

Tribunal in England and Wales (sections 76 to 79 and Third Schedule).

PART VII

ADMINISTRATIVE PROVISIONS

Section 80.

This section *authorizes the Authority to provide special accommodation under its control and management for persons subject to detention under this Act who,* in the Authority's opinion, *require treatment under conditions of special security on account of their dangerous, violent or criminal propensities.*

Section 84.

This section *authorizes the Minister to set up an inquiry* in any case where it appears desirable to do so in connection with any matter arising under this Act.

Annual Reports

Section 85.

This section *requires the Authority and every hospital management committee to include a report of their respective operations under this Act in their annual reports* and every *special care management committee to make annual reports to the Authority on their operations under this Act,* with a copy to the Ministry each year.

Section 87.

This section *requires a management committee, a person carrying on a private hospital and a welfare authority to furnish to the Lord Chief Justice, the Review Tribunal, the Ministry and the Department for the Affairs of Mental Patients such returns,* reports and other information in relation to patients in their care *as are required for the purposes listed in the section.*

PART VIII

FINANCIAL PROVISIONS

Sections 90 and 97 concern various financial matters, including medical practitioners' fares, travelling and subsistence allowances, pocket money for patients and grants to health authorities.

PART IX

MISCELLANEOUS AND GENERAL

Offences

Section 98.

This section *defines offences arising from forgery* or the making of false statements connected with the various processes under the Act which are listed in the section.

The *penalties* for the above offences are, on summary conviction, a term of imprisonment not exceeding six months or a fine not exceeding £100, or both, or, on conviction on indictment, imprisonment for a term not exceeding two years or a fine not exceeding £500, or both.

Ill-Treatment of Patients

Section 100.

This section *renders it an offence for* any officer on the staff or otherwise employed in a hospital, a private hospital, or for any member of the management committee of a hospital or any person running a private hospital to *ill-treat or wilfully neglect a patient receiving treatment* for mental disorder *as an in-patient or on the premises of the hospital or private hospital* while the patient is attending there for treatment for mental disorder *as an out-patient.*

It is also an offence for any individual to ill-treat or wilfully neglect a mentally disordered person while he is subject to his *guardianship* under this Act or in his custody or care.

The *penalties* for the above offences are similar to those in section 98.

Protection of Female Patients

Section 101.

This section *renders it an offence* for any person *to have sexual intercourse with, or commit any of the other acts listed involving a woman detained under this Act* or by order of the Lord Chief Justice *or, not liable to be detained, being a person requiring special care, provided the person charged cannot prove that he did not know and had no reason to know that the woman was within either of these categories.*

The *penalty* for this offence on conviction on indictment is a term of imprisonment not exceeding two years.

Assisting Patients to Absent Themselves Without Leave

Section 102.

This section *renders it an offence to induce or knowingly assist a patient detained in hospital or subject to guardianship under this Act to absent himself without leave,* or to escape from legal custody, or knowingly to harbour a patient absent without leave, or to assist him to prevent, hinder, or interfere with his being taken into custody or returned to hospital or where he should be under guardianship.

The *penalties* for offences under this section are the same as those in section 98.

Warrant to Search for and Remove Patients

Section 105.
This section *authorizes a Justice of the Peace to issue a warrant authorizing a constable to enter,* if need be by force, *any premises specified in the warrant,* and, if thought fit, *to remove from there to a place of safety,* pending arrangements for his treatment or care, *any person whom the Justice of the Peace has,* on information sworn by a welfare officer, by an officer authorized by the Authority or by a constable, *reasonable cause to believe to be suffering from mental disorder and to have been or being ill-treated, neglected, or not kept under proper control and to be living alone and unable to care for himself.* The *constable must be accompanied in the execution of the warrant by a medical practitioner.*

This section also *authorizes a Justice of the Peace,* on information sworn by a welfare officer, by an officer authorized by the Authority or by a constable, *to issue a warrant authorizing any named constable, accompanied by a medical practitioner, to enter any premises, if need be by force, and to remove from there any patient liable to be taken or retaken to any place under this Act, provided admission to the premises has been refused or that such refusal is apprehended.*

A *patient* taken to a place of safety under this section *may be detained there for a period not exceeding seventy-two hours.*

A *'place of safety'* is defined as any hospital the management committee of which are willing temporarily to receive persons taken there under this Act, any Royal Ulster Constabulary station or any other suitable place whose occupier is willing temporarily to receive such persons.

Mentally Disordered Persons Found in Public Places

Section 106.
This section *authorizes a constable to remove to a place of safety an apparently mentally disordered person in immediate need of care or control, found by him in a place to which the public have access, provided he considers it necessary in the interests of that person or for the protection of other persons.*

A person removed in this way *may be detained in the place of safety for a period not exceeding seventy-two hours,* so that he may be examined by a medical practitioner, interviewed by a welfare officer and any arrangements made for his treatment or care.

Notification of Nearest Relative

Section 109.

This section *requires the management committee of a hospital* to which a patient has been admitted, other than on an application of his nearest relative, *to inform that relative of his admission as soon as may be practicable.*

Admission of Patients to Specified Hospitals

Section 110.

This section *authorizes the Authority to order* in writing *a patient's admission,* as the result of any duly completed application under Part II of this Act, *to any hospital specified in the order, and imposes a duty on the management committee of that hospital to admit the patient.*

Index

179

191